HIRAGANA & KATAKANA

	a	i	u	e	o
	あ	い	う	え	お
k	か	き	く	け	こ
s	さ	し	す	せ	そ
t	た	ち chi	つ tsu	て	と
n	な	に	ぬ	ね	の
h	は	ひ	ふ fu	へ	ほ
m	ま	み	む	め	も
y	や		ゆ		よ
r	ら	り	る	れ	ろ
w	わ				を o
n	ん n				

	a	i	u	e
g	が	ぎ	ぐ	げ
z	ざ	じ ji	ず	ぜ
d	だ	ぢ ji	づ zu	で

b	ば	び	ぶ	べ
p	ぱ	ぴ	ぷ	ぺ

	a	i	u	e	o
	ア	イ	ウ	エ	オ
k	カ	キ	ク	ケ	コ
s	サ	シ	ス	セ	ソ
t	タ	チ chi	ツ tsu	テ	ト
n	ナ	ニ	ヌ	ネ	ノ
h	ハ	ヒ	フ fu	ヘ	ホ
m	マ	ミ	ム	メ	モ
y	ヤ		ユ		ヨ
r	ラ	リ	ル	レ	ロ
w	ワ				ヲ o
n	ン n				

	a	i	u	e
g	ガ	ギ	グ	ゲ
z	ザ	ジ ji	ズ	ゼ
d	ダ	ヂ ji	ヅ zu	デ

b	バ	ビ	ブ	ベ
p	パ	ピ	プ	ペ

o
ご
ぞ
ど

ぼ
ぽ

	ya	yu	yo
k	きゃ	きゅ	きょ
s	しゃ sha	しゅ shu	しょ sho
c	ちゃ cha	ちゅ chu	ちょ cho
n	にゃ	にゅ	にょ
h	ひゃ	ひゅ	ひょ
m	みゃ	みゅ	みょ

r	りゃ	りゅ	りょ

	ya	yu	yo
g	ぎゃ	ぎゅ	ぎょ
j	じゃ ja	じゅ ju	じょ jo

b	びゃ	びゅ	びょ
p	ぴゃ	ぴゅ	ぴょ

o
ゴ
ゾ
ド

ボ
ポ

	ya	yu	yo
k	キャ	キュ	キョ
s	シャ sha	シュ shu	ショ sho
c	チャ cha	チュ chu	チョ cho
n	ニャ	ニュ	ニョ
h	ヒャ	ヒュ	ヒョ
m	ミャ	ミュ	ミョ

r	リャ	リュ	リョ

	ya	yu	yo
g	ギャ	ギュ	ギョ
j	ジャ ja	ジュ ju	ジョ jo

b	ビャ	ビュ	ビョ
p	ピャ	ピュ	ピョ

JAPANESE FOR BUSY PEOPLE

Kana Workbook for the Revised 3rd Edition

JAPANESE FOR BUSY PEOPLE

Kana Workbook
for the Revised 3rd Edition

Association for Japanese-Language Teaching
AJALT

KODANSHA USA
New York

The Association for Japanese-Language Teaching (AJALT) was recognized as a nonprofit organization by the Ministry of Education in 1977. It was established to meet the practical needs of people who are not necessarily specialists on Japan but who wish to communicate effectively in Japanese. In 1992 AJALT was awarded the Japan Foundation Special Prize. In 2010 it became a public interest incorporated association. AJALT maintains a website at www.ajalt.org.

Published by Kodansha USA, Inc., 451 Park Avenue South, New York, NY 10016

Distributed in the United Kingdom and continental Europe by Kodansha Europe Ltd.

First published in Japan in 1992 by Kodansha International
Second edition 1996 published in Japan by Kodansha International
Third edition 2007 published in Japan by Kodansha International
First US edition 2012 published by Kodansha USA

Printed in Canada
21 20 19 18 12 11 10 9 8 7 6

ISBN: 978-1-56836-401-8

Illustrations by Shinsaku Sumi

CD narration by Yuri Haruta and Howard Colefield

CD recording and editing by the English Language Education Council, Inc.

PHOTO CREDITS © Sachiyo Yasuda

www.kodanshausa.com

CONTENTS

INTRODUCTION

The *Japanese for Busy People* series focuses on teaching Japanese for effective communication. It is the aim of this workbook—designed for students at the beginner level—to help you to master kana (hiragana and katakana) as painlessly and as efficiently as possible. It is hoped, too, that by learning kana you will feel encouraged to foray even further into your studies of the Japanese language.

By teaching the basics of the kana syllabaries, this book will enable you to better acquire the rhythms and sounds of Japanese speech, thus improving your oral command of the language. The reading and writing abilities gained through the study of kana will, moreover, help to enhance your overall communication skills.

Many of the vocabulary items and expressions in this workbook have been taken from *Japanese for Busy People I: Revised 3rd Edition*. You can use the *Romanized Version* of that text in tandem with this workbook, or you can complete the workbook before embarking on the *Kana Version*. In any case, a mastery of hiragana and katakana is essential for anyone planning to use either *Japanese for Busy People I: Revised 3rd Edition, Kana Version* or *Japanese for Busy People II: Revised 3rd Edition*, since those books use kana and kanji exclusively—that is, without the aid of romanized Japanese.

Overview of the Book

Before going straight into the workbook itself, you may find it worthwhile getting a general idea of its contents. The remainder of this introduction is devoted to that. Note first of all, however, that there is a kana table on pages ii and iii showing all the hiragana and katakana along with their pronunciations.

Introduction to the Japanese Writing System

This section gives an overview of the Japanese writing system, providing some cultural background to capture your interest, while also showing how the kana that you are about to learn fit into and function within Japanese orthography as a whole.

Introduction to the Japanese Sound System

Here you will be introduced to the sounds of Japanese along with the hiragana and katakana used to represent them. Samples of each sound may also be heard on the CD.

Hiragana

This part of the book explains how to write Japanese sounds in hiragana, proceeding from voiceless and voiced consonants to p-sounds, contracted sounds, long vowels, double consonants, and combinations of contracted sounds and long vowels. Lessons on each category of sound move step by step from recognition, reading, and writing of individual characters to reading and writing of entire words. In this way, the book allows you to acquire hiragana logically and efficiently.

Both in this hiragana section and in the katakana one that follows, spaces for practicing individual kana come with reference lines to help you get a feel for the proper size and shape of each character. By thus learning the correct angles and spaces between strokes, you will be able to master even confusingly similar-looking characters and make full use of them in reading and writing.

The Reading Challenge sections starting on page 38 present labeled, picture dictionary–like illustrations of place names, foods, familiar items, and other vocabulary related to daily life in Japan. These pages are intended to provide you with a fun way to practice reading hiragana. Answers can be found at the back of the book.

Starting from page 48 are short reading exercises that present elementary Japanese sentences written in hiragana. Practice reading the sentences, paying particular attention to the irregular readings of hiragana used to write particles.

Katakana

The lessons on katakana open by introducing several katakana with shapes similar to their hiragana counterparts, followed by an overview of the entire katakana syllabary that uses the kana table to relate the characters to the hiragana learned earlier.

As with hiragana, discussion of katakana proceeds from voiceless and voiced consonants to p-sounds, contracted sounds, long vowels, double consonants, and combinations of contracted sounds with long vowels, moving you efficiently from recognizing and writing individual characters to reading and writing whole words.

One function of katakana is to transliterate foreign words into Japanese. As you look through the vocabulary in the lessons, you will gradually come to see what katakana are used to correspond to what sounds in English or other foreign languages. Listen to the CD to familiarize yourself with how the transliterations alter the original sounds to fit Japanese pronunciation.

Illustrated Reading Challenges appear in this part of the book, too. Here, however, different types of words are taken up—mostly loanwords taken from Book I, including country and city names, words for articles of clothing and foods, and other familiar items brought into Japan from the West. Again, the answers are at the back of the book.

Also provided is a section that invites you to learn about and guess at the meanings of various interesting types of katakana words, for example onomatopoeic and mimetic words, contractions, and Japanese-coined words based on English.

The final page of the book, Comprehensive Reading Challenge, will call upon you to bring together everything that you have learned by practicing reading words and sentences written in both hiragana and katakana.

Note: All exercises recorded on the CD are marked with a 

icon.

INTRODUCTION TO THE JAPANESE WRITING SYSTEM

Four Types of Characters

As you walk around Japan or leaf through Japanese books or newspapers, you will notice that Japanese orthography employs several different sets of characters, including the Latin alphabet as well as some others of differing degrees of complexity.

Kanji, the oldest of the four, comes from China and is logographic, with each character representing one unit of meaning. Kanji were introduced into Japan sometime around the sixth century.

Hiragana and katakana were developed in Japan based on kanji, in order to represent the sounds of Japanese. Pure syllabic symbols, they carry none of the meanings originally conveyed by the kanji from which they derive.

Japanese today uses a mixture of kanji logograms and kana sound symbols. The bulk of Japanese writing is done in kanji and hiragana. Katakana is used primarily for words borrowed from foreign languages, though it is also used for onomatopoeia, mimetic words, and scientific names of animals and plants as well as for indicating emphasis.

Finally, romanization, while at first glance much like English, is a system for transliterating sounds in Japanese according to set rules.

In Japanese prose, hiragana typically takes a supporting role as *okurigana* (suffixes that show the inflected endings of verbs or adjectives) or as particles indicating sentence structure. Kanji, meanwhile, are used to write nouns and stems of verbs, adjectives, and adverbs. Hiragana can also be written alongside, above, or beneath kanji to indicate reading, making it a convenient tool for helping learners grow familiar with different characters. Hiragana used in this way is called *rubi* or *furigana*.

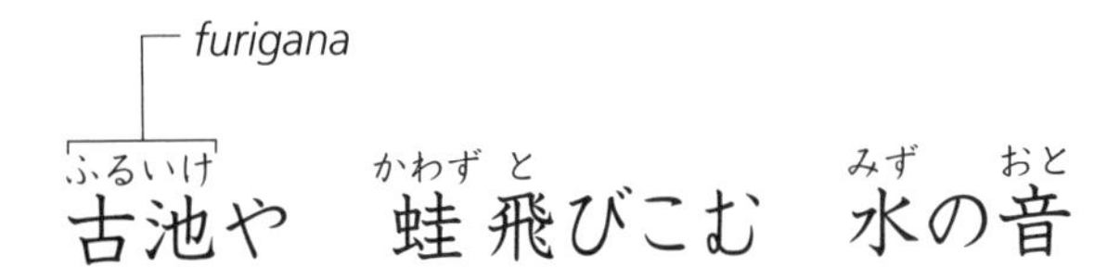

Japanese was traditionally written vertically, from right to left. Along with the influx of Western writing, however, it also came to be written horizontally, from left to right. Today, both systems are equally well used.

Typing in Japanese

On computers with Japanese word-processing functions, users first type in words through keyboards set to accept input either in hiragana or in romanization. After entering a word, users select from several screen options to convert the word as desired into kanji, hiragana, katakana, or romanization. Complicated as it may sound, this method is the one most commonly used for writing e-mails or instant messages in Japanese.

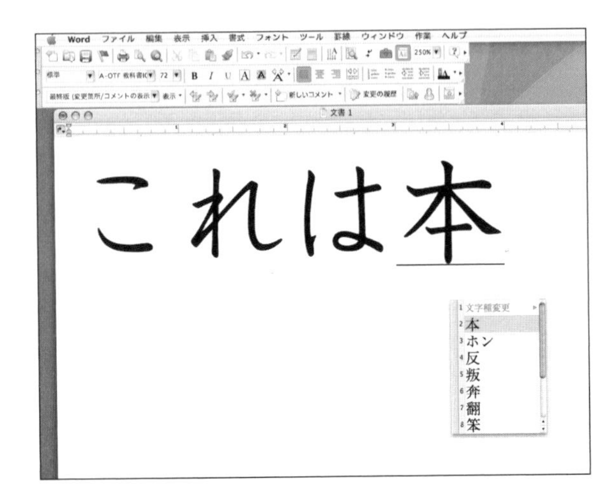

Learning Characters

In Japanese elementary schools, children first learn hiragana, then katakana, then gradually move on to study kanji. As they begin to learn kanji, they start writing what words they can, using the characters they know. Children study about one to two hundred new kanji a year, meanwhile sounding out and learning unfamiliar characters with the aid of *furigana*.

The following pages will introduce you to the two syllabaries of hiragana and katakana as a first step to learning how to write in Japanese.

INTRODUCTION TO THE JAPANESE SOUND SYSTEM

The Japanese phonetic system is composed of five vowel sounds and a number of consonants that combine with these vowels. Each vowel or consonant-vowel combination is one syllable in length, and can be written in either hiragana or katakana.

BASIC SYLLABLES

The Vowels

a	i	u	e	o
あ	い	う	え	お
ア	イ	ウ	エ	オ

The first line of the syllabary consists of the five vowels: *a, i, u, e,* and *o.* They are short vowels, enunciated clearly and crisply. Pronounce the English sentence below, making all of the vowels short, and you will have the approximate sounds.

Ah, we soon get old.
a i u e o

The *u* is pronounced without moving the lips forward. The *o* is similar to the initial sound of "old" but it is not a diphthong, so do not round your lips when you pronounce it.

Consonant-vowel combinations and *n*

The rest of the syllabary consists of syllables formed by a consonant and a vowel. Most Japanese consonants are pronounced with the lips or the tip of the tongue more relaxed than in English. For example, if the *t* in *kite*, as in *kite kudasai* (please come), is pronounced too strongly and with a good deal of aspiration, it will be heard as *kitte* (stamp), an entirely different word. So be especially careful to pronounce *p, t,* and *k* with less aspiration than in English.

	a	i	u	e	o
k	か	き	く	け	こ
	カ	キ	ク	ケ	コ
g	が	ぎ	ぐ	げ	ご
	ガ	ギ	グ	ゲ	ゴ

The consonant *k* is pronounced more softly than in English.

At the beginning of a word, the *g* in *ga, gi, gu, ge,* or *go* is hard (like the "g" in "garden"), but when occurring in the middle of a word or in the last syllable, it is often nasal, as in *eiga* (movie). The particle *ga*, too, is usually nasalized, though nowadays many people use a hard *g* when pronouncing it.

	a	i	u	e	o
s	さ	し	す	せ	そ
		shi			
	サ	シ	ス	セ	ソ
z	ざ	じ	ず	ぜ	ぞ
		ji			
	ザ	ジ	ズ	ゼ	ゾ

The breath is expelled less forcefully when pronouncing this consonant in Japanese than in English. *Shi* is a near equivalent of the English "she" but is enunciated with the lips unrounded. Note that there is no Japanese syllable *si*.

The breath is expelled less forcefully with this Japanese consonant than with the English one. When *za*, *zu*, *ze*, or *zo* come at the beginning of a word, the *z* is affricative, sounding like "ds" in "kids." In the middle of a word or in the last syllable, however, it is fricative, sounding like the "z" in "zoo." *Ji* is an affricate at the beginning of a word, like the "je" in "jeep," but fricative in a middle position, like "si" in "vision." Note that Japanese does not have the syllable *zi*.

	a	i	u	e	o
t	た	ち	つ	て	と
		chi	tsu		
	タ	チ	ツ	テ	ト
d	だ	ぢ	づ	で	ど
		ji	zu		
	ダ	ヂ	ヅ	デ	ド

The aspiration of this consonant is weaker than its English counterpart. *Chi* is pronounced like "chi" in "children." *Tsu* is pronounced with the consonant *ts* similar to the "ts" in "cats." Note that Japanese does not have the syllables *ti* or *tu*.

ぢ and づ are pronounced *ji* and *zu*. (The syllables *di* and *du* do not exist.) In general, *ji* and *zu* are written じ and ず, respectively, but in a few rare cases custom calls for ぢ and づ.

	a	i	u	e	o
n	な	に	ぬ	ね	の
	ナ	ニ	ヌ	ネ	ノ

This consonant is similar to the "n" in "nice" but is less prolonged.

	a	i	u	e	o
h	は	ひ	ふ	へ	ほ
			fu		
	ハ	ヒ	フ	ヘ	ホ
b	ば	び	ぶ	べ	ぼ
	バ	ビ	ブ	ベ	ボ
p	ぱ	ぴ	ぷ	ぺ	ぽ
	パ	ピ	プ	ペ	ポ

The breath is not expelled as strongly as in English. In *fu*, the consonant is not made the same way as the "f" in the English word "foot." It is produced by expelling air through lightly compressed lips, much like blowing out a candle.

This consonant is pronounced nearly the same as the English "b."

This consonant is pronounced with less aspiration than the English "p."

	a	i	u	e	o
m	ま マ	み ミ	む ム	め メ	も モ

This consonant is similar to the "m" in "mind," though not quite as long.

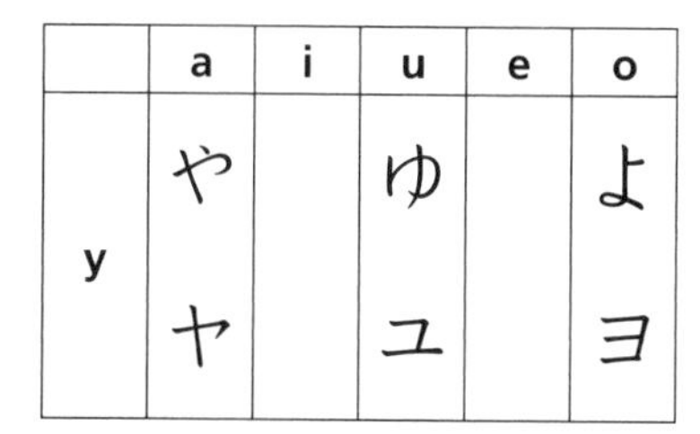

	a	i	u	e	o
y	や ヤ		ゆ ユ		よ ヨ

The Japanese *y* is pronounced with the tongue in a more relaxed position than for the "y" of "year."

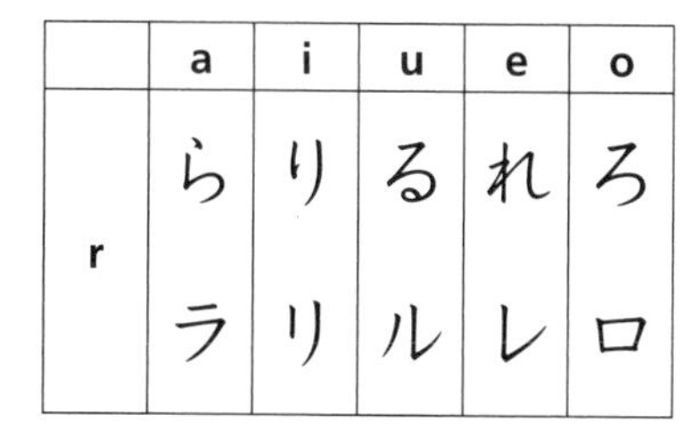

	a	i	u	e	o
r	ら ラ	り リ	る ル	れ レ	ろ ロ

The Japanese *r* is produced by tapping the tip of the tongue lightly against the teethridge. It is never pronounced with the tip of the tongue curled back.

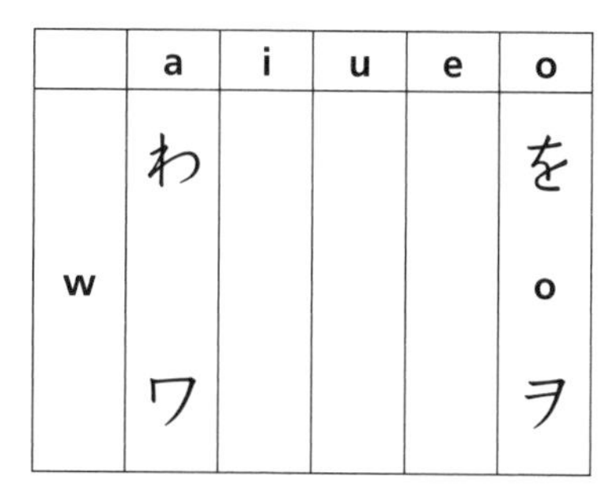

	a	i	u	e	o
w	わ ワ				を o ヲ

W is pronounced with the lips rounded, but not so tightly or forcefully as for the "w" in "wait." を and ヲ used to be pronounced *wo* but are now pronounced *o*.

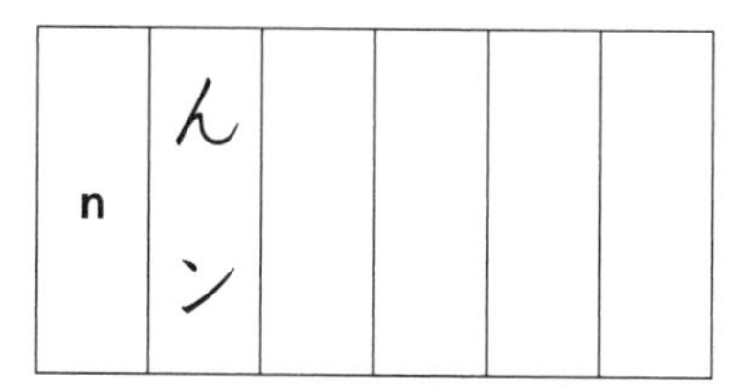

n	ん ン				

N is the only consonant not combined with a vowel. Occurring at the end of a word, it has a somewhat nasal sound. Otherwise it approximates the English "n." If it is followed by syllables beginning with *b*, *m*, or *p*, however, it is pronounced more like "m" and accordingly is spelled with "m" in this book.

Special care is needed when the syllable *n* is followed by a vowel, as in the word *kin'en* (*ki-n-en*, "no smoking"). Note the difference in syllable division between this word and *kinen* (*ki-ne-n*, "anniversary").

MODIFIED SYLLABLES

Consonants plus *ya*, *yu*, or *yo*

Although the following are each written with two hiragana or katakana characters, they are pronounced as single syllables. The *y*, which sounds like the "y" in "year," is pronounced between the initial consonant and the following vowel.

	ya	yu	yo
k	きゃ キャ	きゅ キュ	きょ キョ
g	ぎゃ ギャ	ぎゅ ギュ	ぎょ ギョ
s	しゃ sha シャ	しゅ shu シュ	しょ sho ショ
j	じゃ ja ジャ	じゅ ju ジュ	じょ jo ジョ
c	ちゃ cha チャ	ちゅ chu チュ	ちょ cho チョ
n	にゃ ニャ	にゅ ニュ	にょ ニョ

	ya	yu	yo
h	ひゃ ヒャ	ひゅ ヒュ	ひょ ヒョ
b	びゃ ビャ	びゅ ビュ	びょ ビョ
p	ぴゃ ピャ	ぴゅ ピュ	ぴょ ピョ
m	みゃ ミャ	みゅ ミュ	みょ ミョ
r	りゃ リャ	りゅ リュ	りょ リョ

OTHER SYLLABLES

Long Vowels

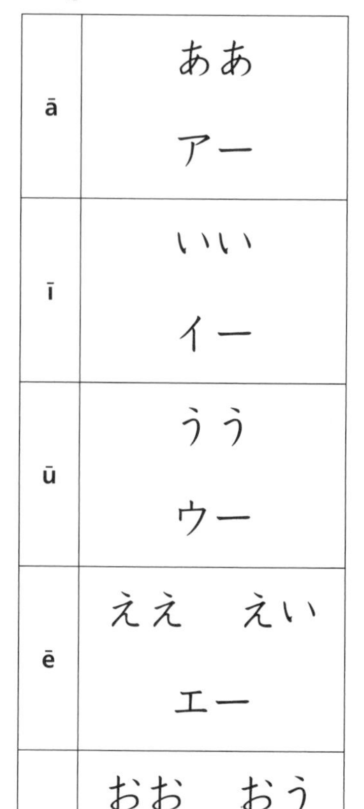

ā	ああ アー
ī	いい イー
ū	うう ウー
ē	ええ　えい エー
ō	おお　おう オー

Long vowels, indicated in romanized Japanese with a macron [¯], represent a doubling of single vowels. Be particularly careful to pronounce them as a continuous sound, equal in value to two short vowels. The way long vowels are written varies from case to case. With *ā*, *ī*, *ū*, the single vowel is simply doubled: ああ, いい, うう. *Ee* is most often written えい, though ええ is also seen. *Ō* is generally おう, but some words customarily demand おお. The same rules apply when a consonant is followed by a long vowel: e.g., *kā* (かあ), *kī* (きい), *kū* (くう), *kē* (けい, けえ), *kō* (こう, こお).

Double Consonants

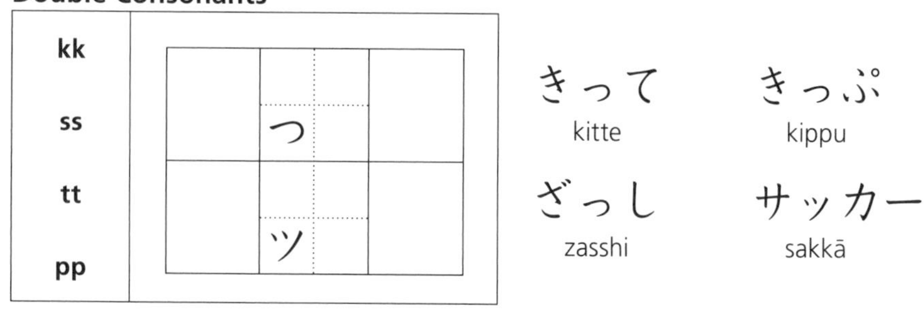

The first consonant of the double consonants *kk*, *ss*, *tt*, and *pp* is written with a small っ. The っ here indicates a one-syllable pause, during which the mouth prepares itself for the pronunciation of the next syllable. Take *kitte*, for example. After pronouncing *ki*, pause for the length of one syllable, shaping your mouth for the pronunciation of *te*, and then pronounce it—*te*. With *ss*, as in *zasshi*, see that a small amount of air is emitted between the teeth before pronouncing the following syllable.

HIRAGANA

BASIC SYLLABLES

Recognition of Forms

あいうえお　かきくけこ　さしすせそ

Identify the syllables in parentheses from among the ones listed to the right.

I.
(あ) ゆ お よ あ ぬ お
a
(い) い に こ い り い
i
(う) え う ろ ら う ら
u
(え) ん え よ ん く え
e
(お) あ よ は お ま お
o

II.
(か) が か け が あ か
ka
(き) ま さ き ざ き ぎ
ki
(く) し へ く ぐ し く
ku
(け) は け ほ げ は け
ke
(こ) こ い に い ご こ
ko

III.
(さ) き さ ざ せ さ き
sa
(し) く し へ ん じ し
shi
(す) ま す む よ す ず
su
(せ) せ さ や ぜ さ や
se
(そ) え そ ろ ぞ ら そ
so

IV.
(あ) (い) (う) あ り こ い あ ろ う ら こ お い う お あ い
a i u
(き) (く) (え) さ し え き ぐ ん ぎ く へ く き さ え べ き
ki ku e
(す) (そ) (お) ま ろ そ よ す あ ず そ お ろ す お あ そ す
su so o
(せ) (け) (か) や せ は け ほ が か お に け ぜ か け や せ
se ke ka

Reading (answers given below)

1. あか　2. いえ　3. かぐ　4. しお　5. かぎ　6. あお

1. **aka** (red)　2. **ie** (house)　3. **kagu** (furniture)　4. **shio** (salt)　5. **kagi** (key)　6. **ao** (blue)

たちつてと　なにぬねの　はひふへほ

Identify the syllables in parentheses from among the ones listed to the right.

I.
(た) に こ た な に こ
ta

(ち) ろ う る ち ら ち
chi

(つ) し う つ く て つ
tsu

(て) し で こ て く て
te

(と) を と て と ち と
to

II.
(な) た な ば な は な
na

(に) に た こ に い こ
ni

(ぬ) ね め ぬ ぬ な わ
nu

(ね) め わ ね れ ね わ
ne

(の) め の ね の め の
no

III.
(は) ば は ぱ け ま は
ha

(ひ) ぴ ひ び ひ ぴ ひ
hi

(ふ) そ ふ ぷ へ ぶ ふ
fu

(へ) つ へ ぺ く へ べ
he

(ほ) は ま ほ ば ほ ぼ
ho

IV.
(た) (な) (は) に な ほ ば た は け ぼ な た は な た な は
ta na ha

(で) (ど) (べ) と で へ を ど し べ ご ぺ て へ で と ど ぺ
de do be

(て) (に) (の) た の て で に の こ く て に め の に で た
te ni no

(つ) (ぬ) (ち) し め つ ち ら ね へ つ ぬ め し く さ ち ぬ
tsu nu chi

Reading (answers given below)

1. はな　2. おかね　3. さかな　4. いぬ　5. ちかてつ

1. **hana** (flower)　2. **okane** (money)　3. **sakana** (fish)　4. **inu** (dog)　3. **chikatetsu** (subway)

まみむめも　やゆよ　らりるれろ　わをん

Identify the syllables in parentheses from among the ones listed to the right.

I. (ま) よ ま き ま ほ ま
ma

(み) ゆ の み み お み
mi

(む) ぬ す め む す む
mu

(め) の ぬ め あ ぬ め
me

(も) も ま し と も ほ
mo

II. (や) せ や せ さ や せ
ya

(ゆ) の ゆ る ゆ ひ の
yu

(よ) ま ゆ よ ろ す よ
yo

III. (ら) ろ そ う る ら ち
ra

(り) い り こ り い り
ri

(る) ら る ろ り ら る
ru

(れ) れ わ ね れ わ め
re

(ろ) そ ろ ら ち ろ ら
ro

IV. (わ) れ わ ね め あ わ
wa

(を) と を と を て を
o

(ん) ん え て ん え ん
n

V. (ま) (よ) (も) お ま ほ も ば よ す よ き ま も お も ま も
ma yo mo

(ら) (ろ) (る) る そ う ら ろ ち る え ら み ろ ら お ろ る
ra ro ru

(め) (わ) (れ) れ ぬ め ね わ む め ま ろ わ を れ め ね あ
me wa re

(を) (と) (て) さ と つ て を き へ て で と ど を て ど へ
o to te

(く) (し) (つ) く ぐ じ つ へ し け じ く つ へ て づ し ぐ
ku shi tsu

(は) (ほ) (ま) ぼ ま は は よ す ほ ば ま け に は ま よ ほ
ha ho ma

Reading (answers given below)

1. やま　2. かわ　3. むら　4. よる　5. みんな

---

1. **yama** (mountain) 2. **kawa** (river) 3. **mura** (village) 4. **yoru** (night) 5. **minna** (everyone)

Writing

The gray lines are aids to accurate style. In writing hiragana, the stroke order is, as a rule, first from top to bottom, then from left to right. To be sure, follow the arrows.

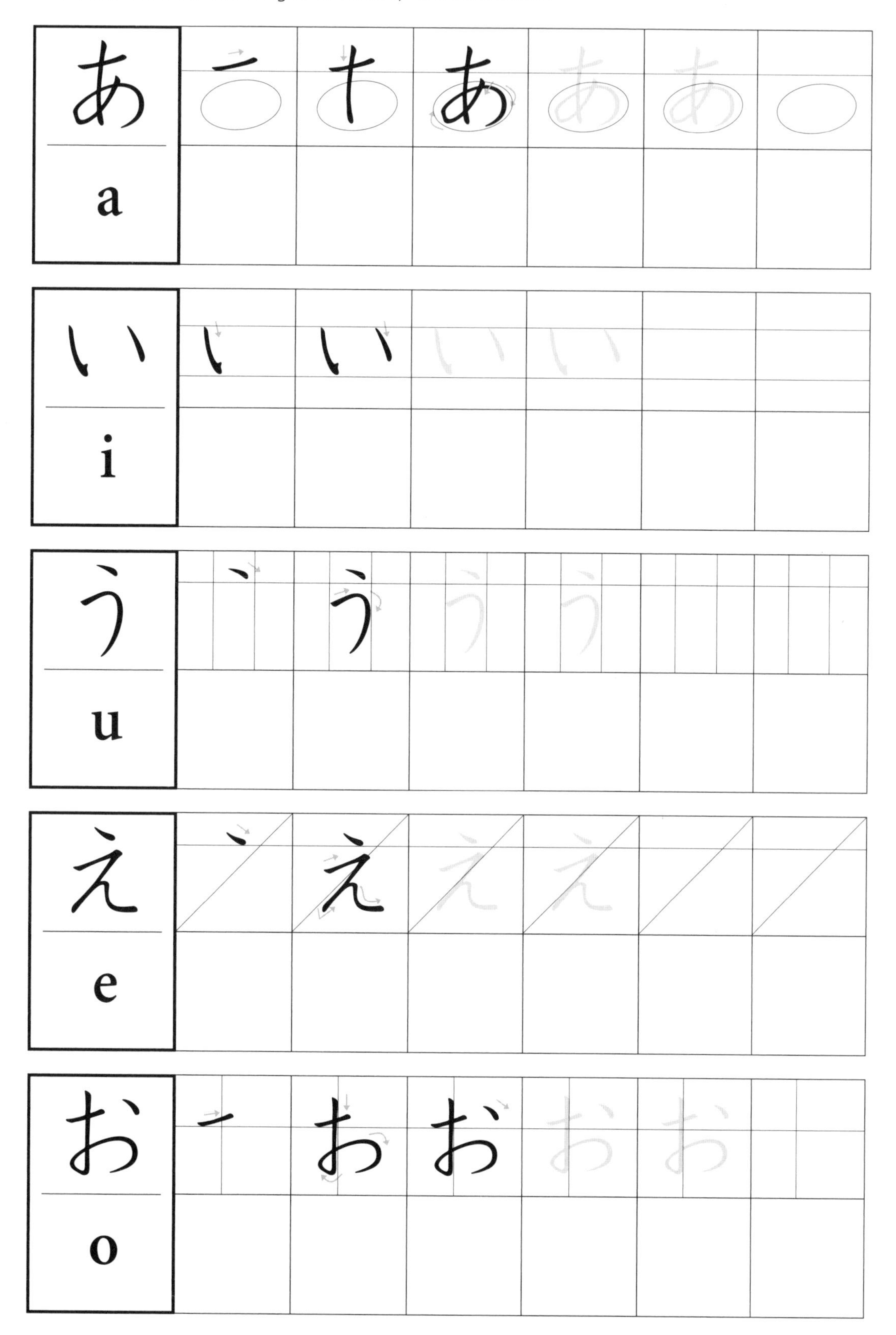

か ka	㇇	カ	か	か	か	
き ki	一	二	キ	き	き	き
く ku	く	く	く			
け ke	l	lー	け	け	け	
こ ko	㇖	こ	こ	こ		

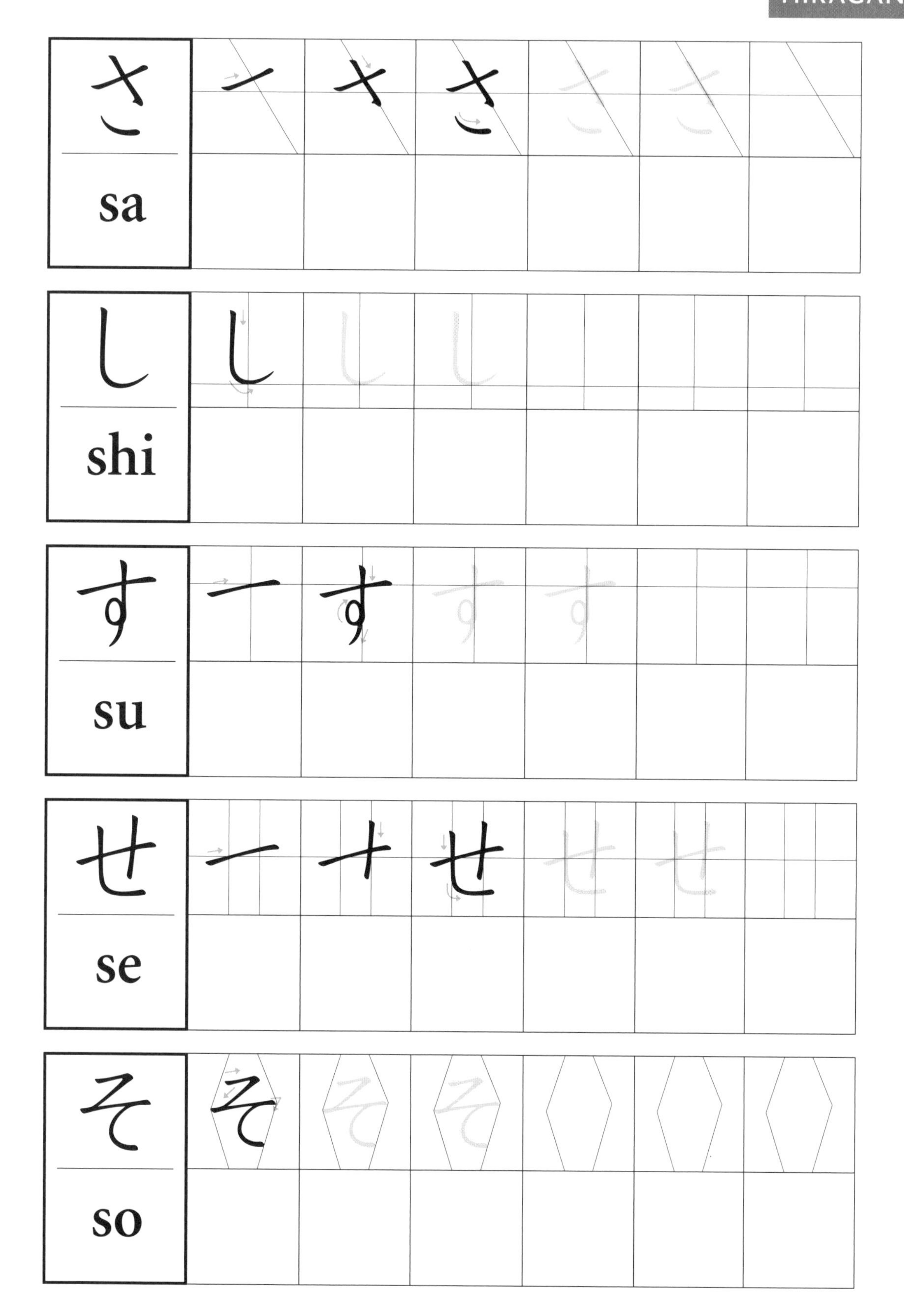
さ
sa
し
shi
す
su
せ
se
そ
so

た ta	ナ	ナ	た	た	た	た

ち chi	一	ち	ち	ち		

つ tsu	つ	つ	つ			

て te	て	て	て			

と to	ヽ	と	と	と		

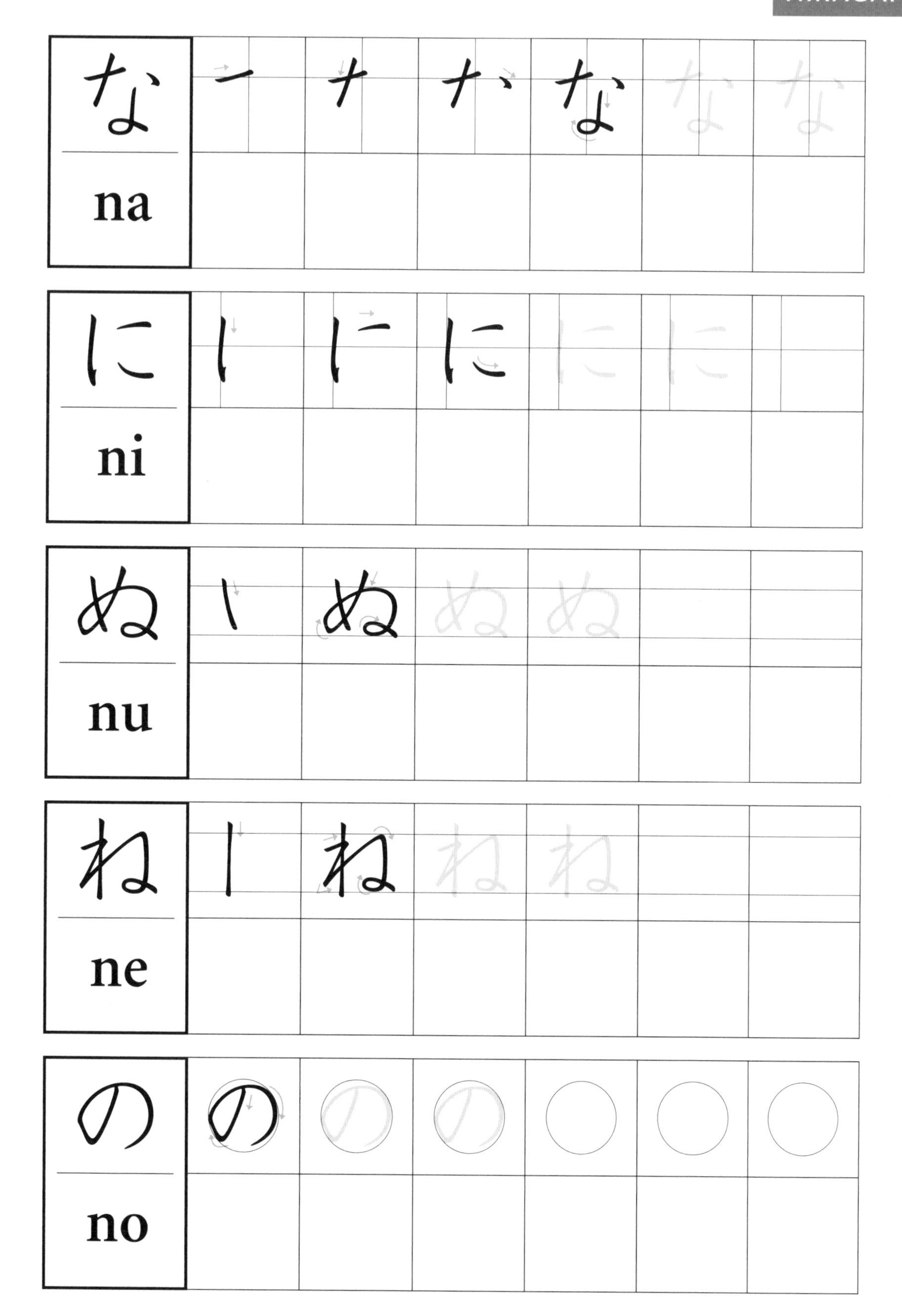
な
na
に
ni
ぬ
nu
ね
ne
の
no

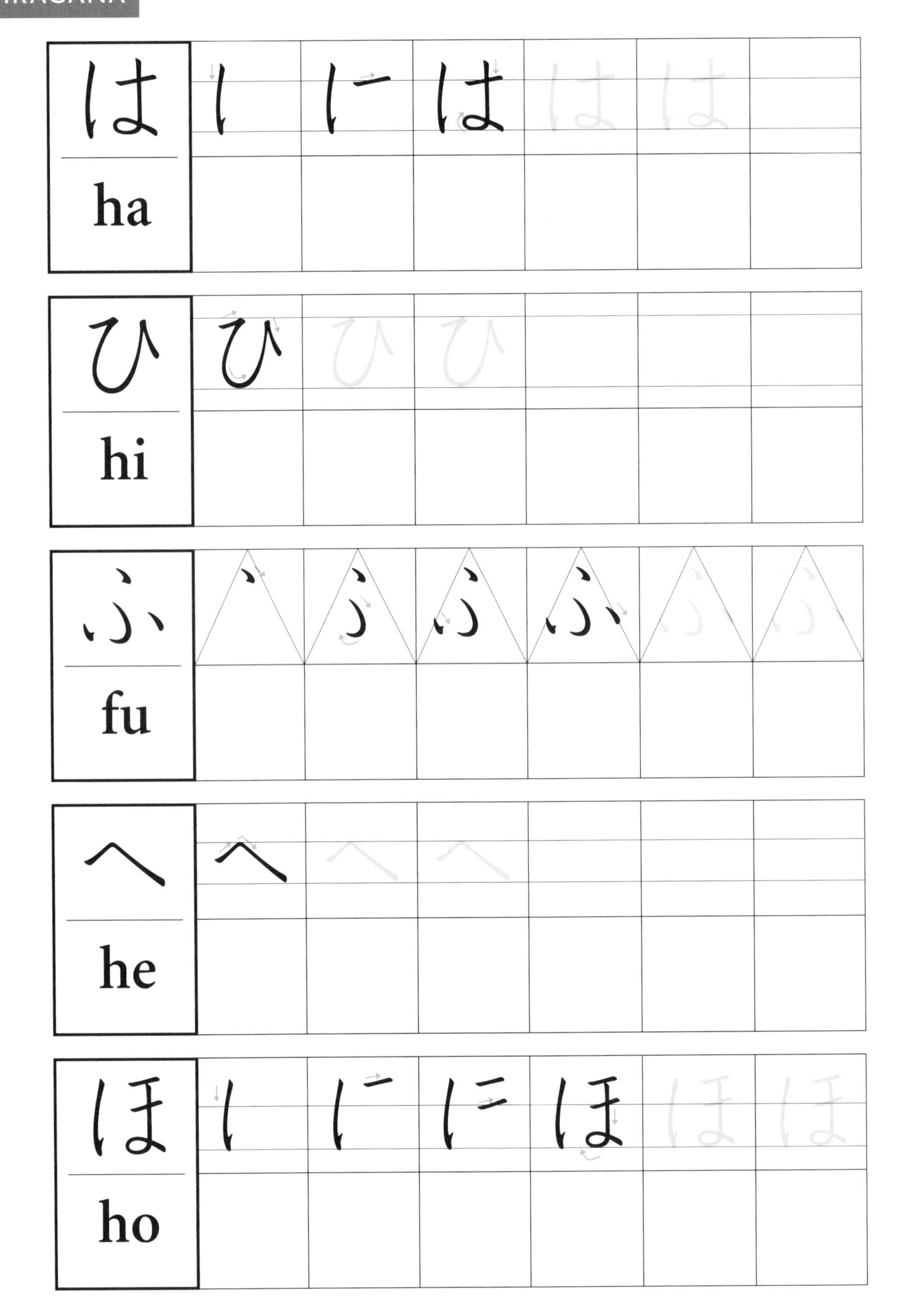
は
ha
ひ
hi
ふ
fu
へ
he
ほ
ho

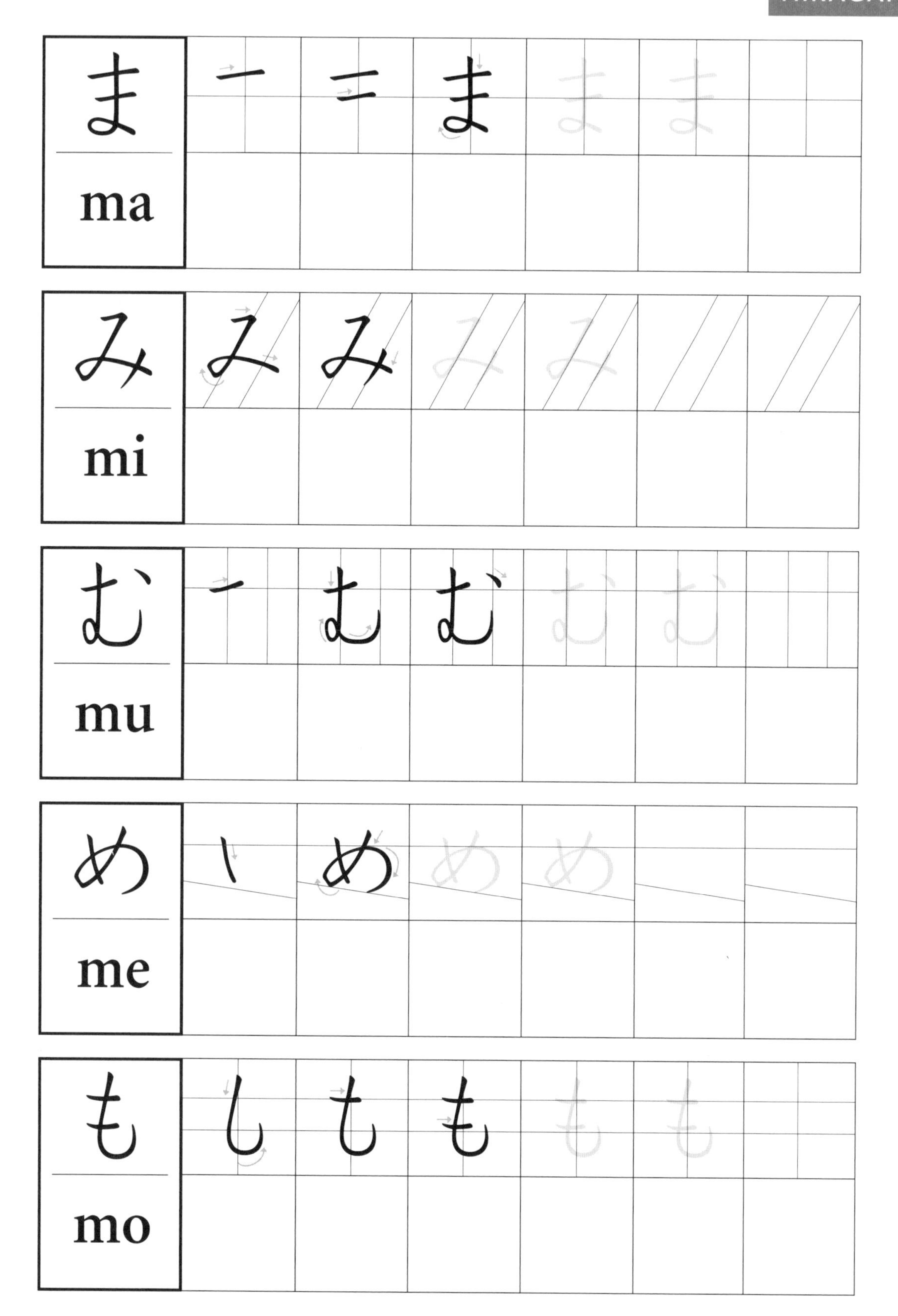
ま
ma
み
mi
む
mu
め
me
も
mo

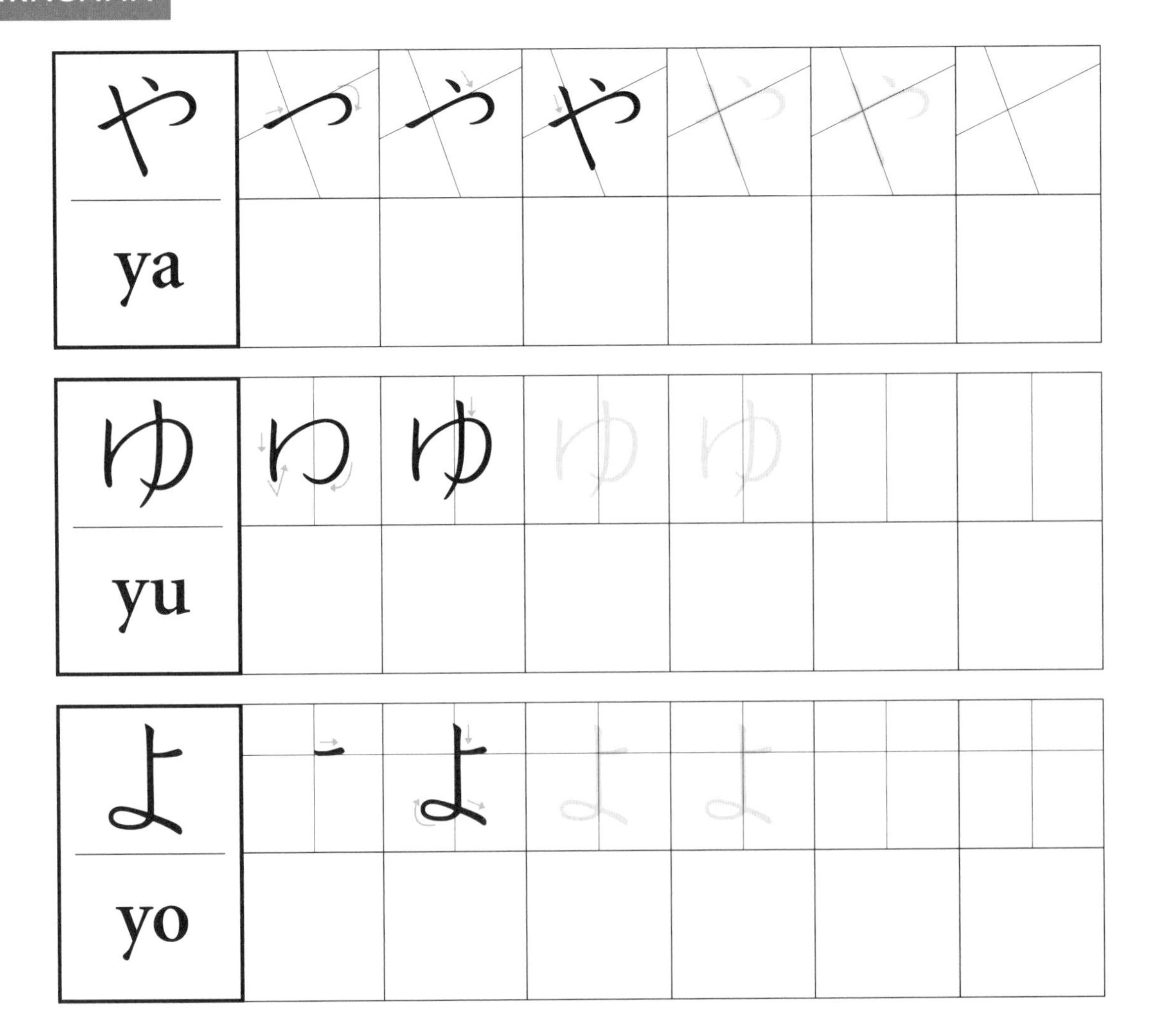
や
ya
ゆ
yu
よ
yo

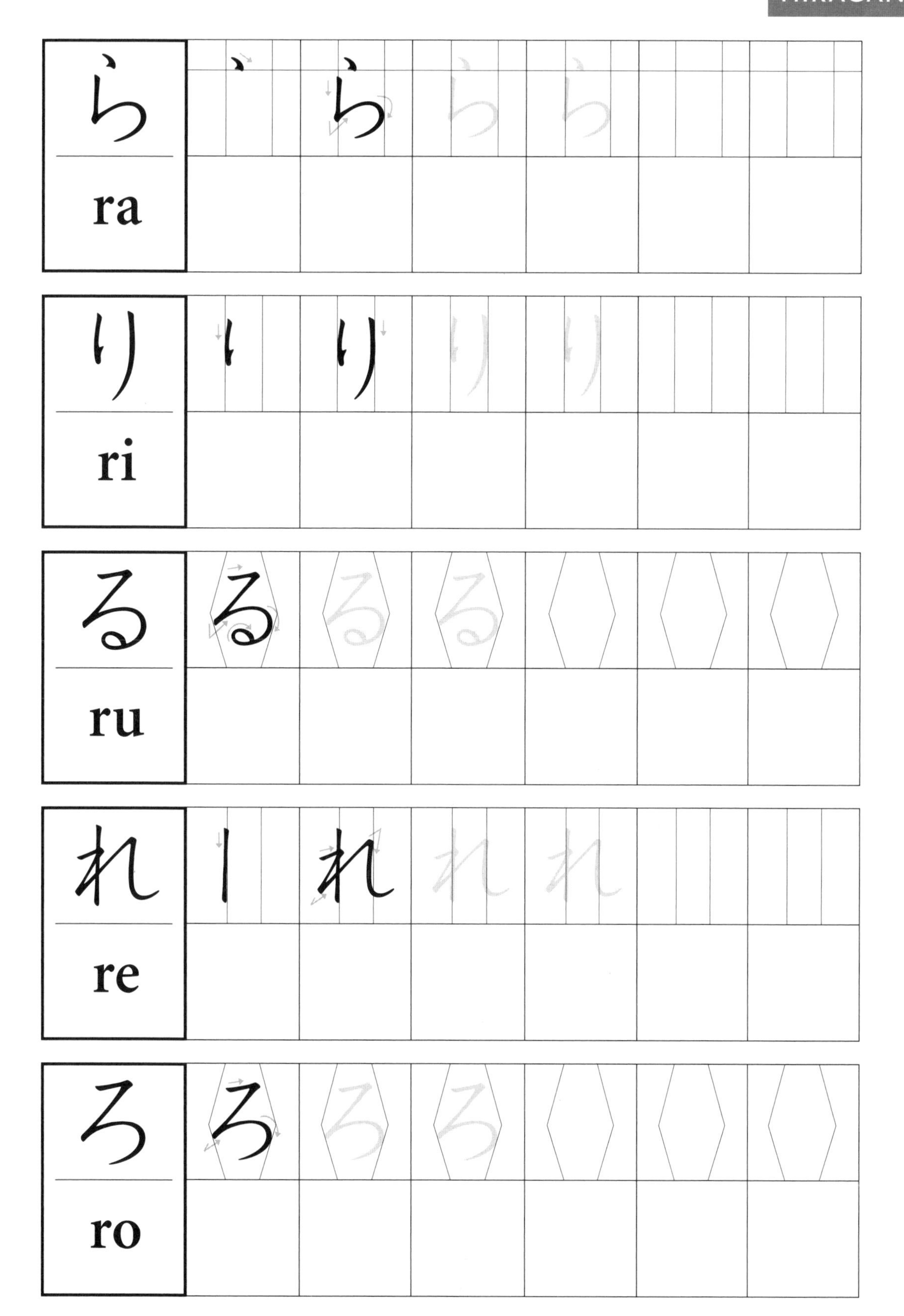
ら
ra
り
ri
る
ru
れ
re
ろ
ro

わ wa		
を o		
ん n		

VOICED & SEMIVOICED SYLLABLES

The (˘) and (°) in が, ぱ, etc., should be written in the upper right-hand corner of the syllable. Write the following hiragana, following the examples.

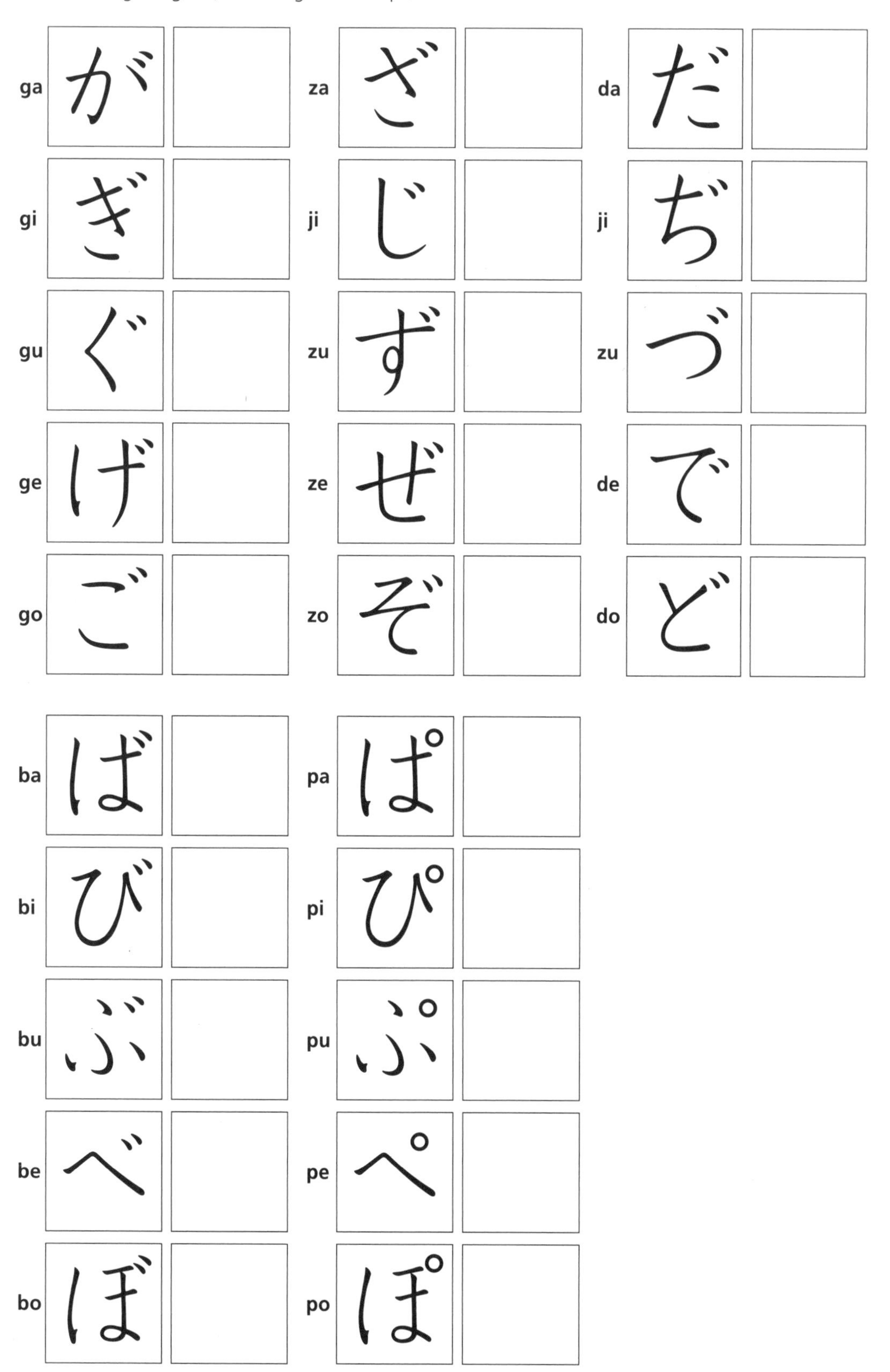

Reading & Writing

First read the words, then write them.

1. うち
2. くるま
3. かさ
4. しごと
5. みず
6. かぎ
7. べんごし
8. なつ
9. ひと
10. ほん
11. でんち
12. みかん

---

1. **uchi** (home) 2. **kuruma** (car) 3. **kasa** (umbrella) 4. **shigoto** (job, work) 5. **mizu** (water) 6. **kagi** (key) 7. **bengoshi** (attorney) 8. **natsu** (summer) 9. **hito** (person) 10. **hon** (book) 11. **denchi** (battery) 12. **mikan** (tangerine)

LOOK-ALIKE HIRAGANA

Some hiragana look alike. Read, write, and distinguish the following pairs of look-alike syllables.

1. あ お
2. き さ
3. ぬ ね
4. て こ
5. し も
6. る ろ
7. ほ は
8. た な 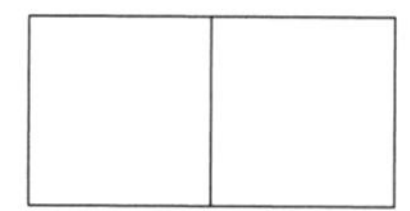
9. つ と
10. う つ 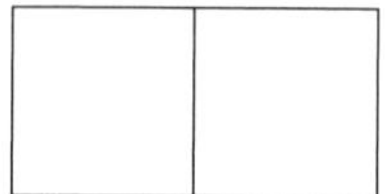
11. こ い 
12. ま ほ
13. め ぬ 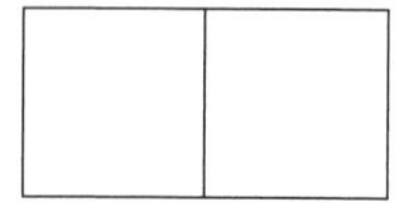
14. へ て 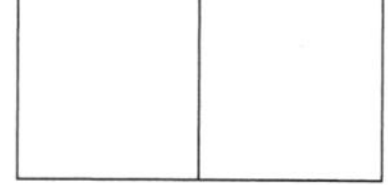
15. り い
16. す む 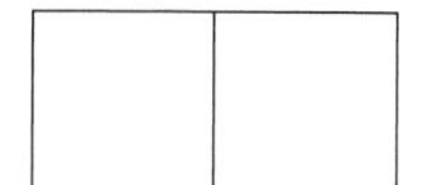
17. え ふ 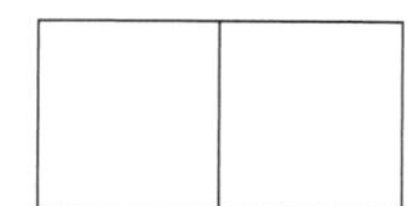
18. そ て 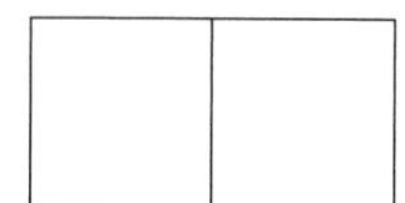

1. **a o** 2. **ki sa** 3. **nu ne** 4. **te ko** 5. **shi mo** 6. **ru ro** 7. **ho ha** 8. **ta na** 9. **tsu to** 10. **u tsu** 11. **ko i** 12. **ma ho** 13. **me nu** 14. **he te** 15. **ri i** 16. **su mu** 17. **e fu** 18. **so te**

MODIFIED SYLLABLES

Recognition of Forms

As you have already learned, a consonant plus a small や, ゆ, or よ is pronounced as a single syllable.

きゃ **kya**	きゅ **kyu**	きょ **kyo**		ぎゃ **gya**	ぎゅ **gyu**	ぎょ **gyo**				
しゃ **sha**	しゅ **shu**	しょ **sho**		じゃ **ja**	じゅ **ju**	じょ **jo**				
ちゃ **cha**	ちゅ **chu**	ちょ **cho**								
にゃ **nya**	にゅ **nyu**	にょ **nyo**								
ひゃ **hya**	ひゅ **hyu**	ひょ **hyo**		びゃ **bya**	びゅ **byu**	びょ **byo**		ぴゃ **pya**	ぴゅ **pyu**	ぴょ **pyo**
みゃ **mya**	みゅ **myu**	みょ **myo**								
りゃ **rya**	りゅ **ryu**	りょ **ryo**								

Identify the syllables in parentheses from among the ones listed to the right.

(きゃ) きゅ ぎゃ ちゃ きゃ きょ みゃ きょ きゅ

(しゅ) じょ しゃ りゃ じゅ ひゃ ちゅ しゅ しょ

(ちょ) ちゅ にょ みょ しゅ ちょ ちゃ きゅ ひゃ

(にゅ) しゅ ひゅ にょ びょ にゅ にゃ みゅ みょ

Reading (answers given below)

1. かいしゃ 2. おちゃ 3. ひゃく 4. りょかん 5. うんてんしゅ

---

1. **kaisha** (company) 2. **o-cha** (green tea) 3. **hyaku** (one hundred) 4. **ryokan** (traditional Japanese inn) 5. **untenshu** (driver)

Writing

A consonant plus a small ゃ, ゅ, or ょ is written with two hiragana characters and occupies the space of two characters. Small ゃ, ゅ, and ょ are written approximately one-forth the size of a normal character. In horizontal writing, they appear small in the lower left quadrant of the square.

ja	じ	ゃ
ju	じ	ゅ
jo	じ	ょ

cha	ち	ゃ
chu	ち	ゅ
cho	ち	ょ

nya	に	ゃ
nyu	に	ゅ
nyo	に	ょ

hya	ひ	ゃ
hyu	ひ	ゅ
hyo	ひ	ょ

bya	び	や						
byu	び	ゆ						
byo	び	よ						

pya	ぴ	や						
pyu	ぴ	ゆ						
pyo	ぴ	よ						

mya	み	や						
myu	み	ゆ						
myo	み	よ						

rya	り	や						
ryu	り	ゆ						
ryo	り	よ						

LONG VOWELS

Reading

ā	ああ	ī	いい	ū	うう	ē	ええ　えい	ō	おお　おう

Sound out the following words, being careful to pronounce the long vowels correctly.

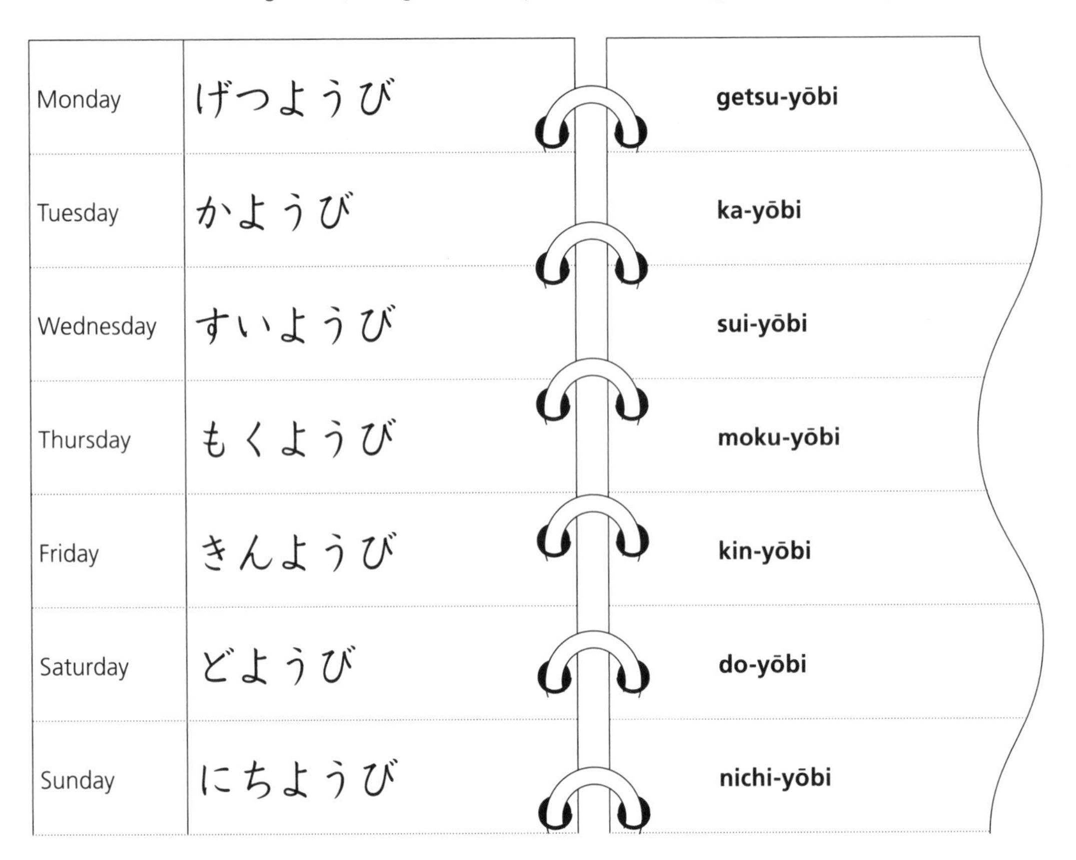

Monday	げつようび	getsu-yōbi
Tuesday	かようび	ka-yōbi
Wednesday	すいようび	sui-yōbi
Thursday	もくようび	moku-yōbi
Friday	きんようび	kin-yōbi
Saturday	どようび	do-yōbi
Sunday	にちようび	nichi-yōbi

Reading

Practice more long vowels by describing your family. The words in parentheses are occupations.

1. **otōsan** father (**kaikeishi** accountant) 2. **okāsan** mother (**sensei** teacher) 3. **onīsan** elder brother (**haiyū** actor) 4. **onēsan** elder sister (**ginkōin** banker) 5. **watashi** me, myself 6. **otōto** younger brother (**gakusei** student) 7. **imōto** younger sister (**gakusei** student)

Writing

1. げつようび

2. かようび

3. おとうさん

4. おかあさん

5. おにいさん

6. おねえさん

7. せんせい

8. ひこうき

9. とけい

10. とお

1. **getsu-yōbi** (Monday) 2. **ka-yōbi** (Tuesday) 3. **otōsan** (father) 4. **okāsan** (mother) 5. **onīsan** (elder brother) 6. **onēsan** (elder sister) 7. **sensei** (teacher) 8. **hikōki** (airplane) 9. **tokei** (watch, clock) 10. **tō** (ten)

DOUBLE CONSONANTS

Reading

kk ss tt pp	っ

As you have already learned, the first consonant of a double consonant (*kk*, *ss*, *tt*, or *pp*) is written with a small っ. Read the words below, taking care to pronounce the double consonants properly.

1. ひとつ
2. ふたつ
3. みっつ
4. よっつ
5. いつつ
6. むっつ
7. ななつ
8. やっつ
9. ここのつ

---

1. **hitotsu** (one) 2. **futatsu** (two) 3. **mittsu** (three) 4. **yottsu** (four) 5. **itsutsu** (five) 6. **muttsu** (six) 7. **nanatsu** (seven) 8. **yattsu** (eight) 9. **kokonotsu** (nine)

Writing

1. ひとつ
2. ふたつ
3. みっつ
4. よっつ
5. いつつ
6. むっつ
7. ななつ
8. やっつ
9. ここのつ
10. いっぽん
11. いっぷん
12. ざっし
13. きって
14. きっぷ

---

1. **hitotsu** (one) 2. **futatsu** (two) 3. **mittsu** (three) 4. **yottsu** (four) 5. **itsutsu** (five) 6. **muttsu** (six) 7. **nanatsu** (seven) 8. **yattsu** (eight) 9. **kokonotsu** (nine) 10. **ippon** (one [when counting long, slender items]) 11. **ippun** (one minute) 12. **zasshi** (magazine) 13. **kitte** (stamp) 14. **kippu** (ticket)

COMBINATIONS OF MODIFIED AND OTHER SYLLABLES

Reading

1. きょう
2. てちょう
3. りょうり
4. しゅうまつ
5. じゅうしょ
6. ゆうびんきょく
7. とうきょう
8. ちゅうごく
9. しゃちょう
10. りょこう
11. びょういん
12. たんじょうび
13. しゅっちょう
14. りょうしゅうしょ
15. ちゅうしゃじょう

---

1. **kyō** (today) 2. **techō** (datebook) 3. **ryōri** (cooking) 4. **shūmatsu** (weekend) 5. **jūsho** (address) 6. **yūbinkyoku** (post office) 7. **Tōkyō** (Tokyo) 8. **Chūgoku** (China) 9. **shachō** (company president) 10. **ryokō** (trip, travel) 11. **byōin** (hospital) 12. **tanjōbi** (birthday) 13. **shutchō** (business trip) 14. **ryōshūsho** (receipt) 15. **chūshajō** (parking lot)

Writing

1. いっぷん

2. じゅうしょ

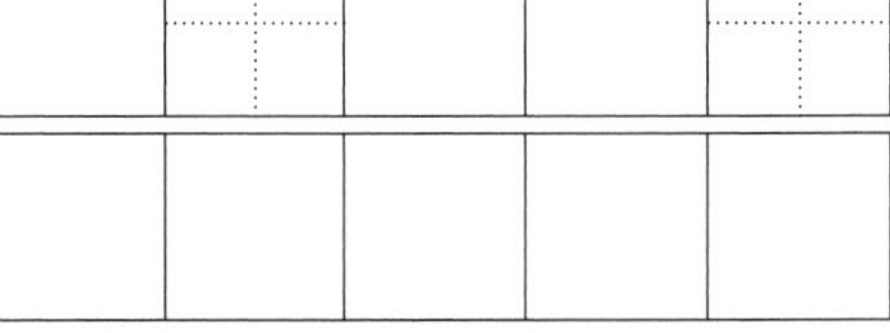

3. しゅっちょう

4. りょこう

5. ひしょ

6. でんしゃ

7. たんじょうび

8. とうきょう

9. 5じ10ぷん

5		10		
5		10		

1. **ippun** (one minute) 2. **jūsho** (address) 3.**shutchō** (business trip) 4. **ryokō** (trip, travel) 5. **hisho** (secretary) 6.**densha** (train) 7. **tanjōbi** (birthday) 8. **Tōkyō** (Tokyo) 9. **go-ji juppun** (5:10)

VERTICAL LAYOUT

The small や, ゆ, and よ in modified syllables, and the small っ that indicates a double consonant, are written in different quadrants according to whether the text is horizontal or vertical. As we have seen, in horizontal writing they appear in the lower left quadrant of the square. In vertical writing they appear in the upper right quadrant.

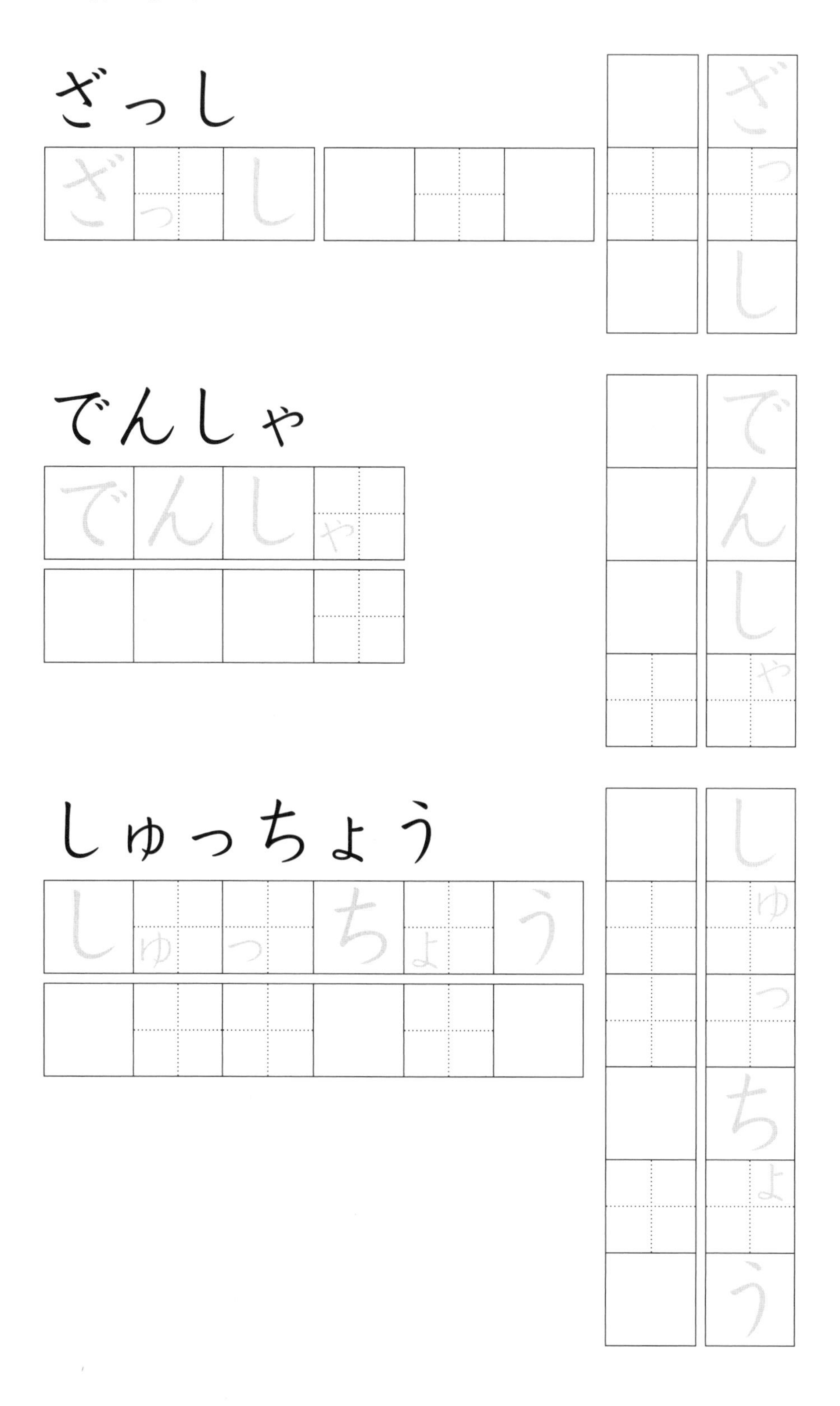

READING CHALLENGE 1: Japan

(answers on p. 85)

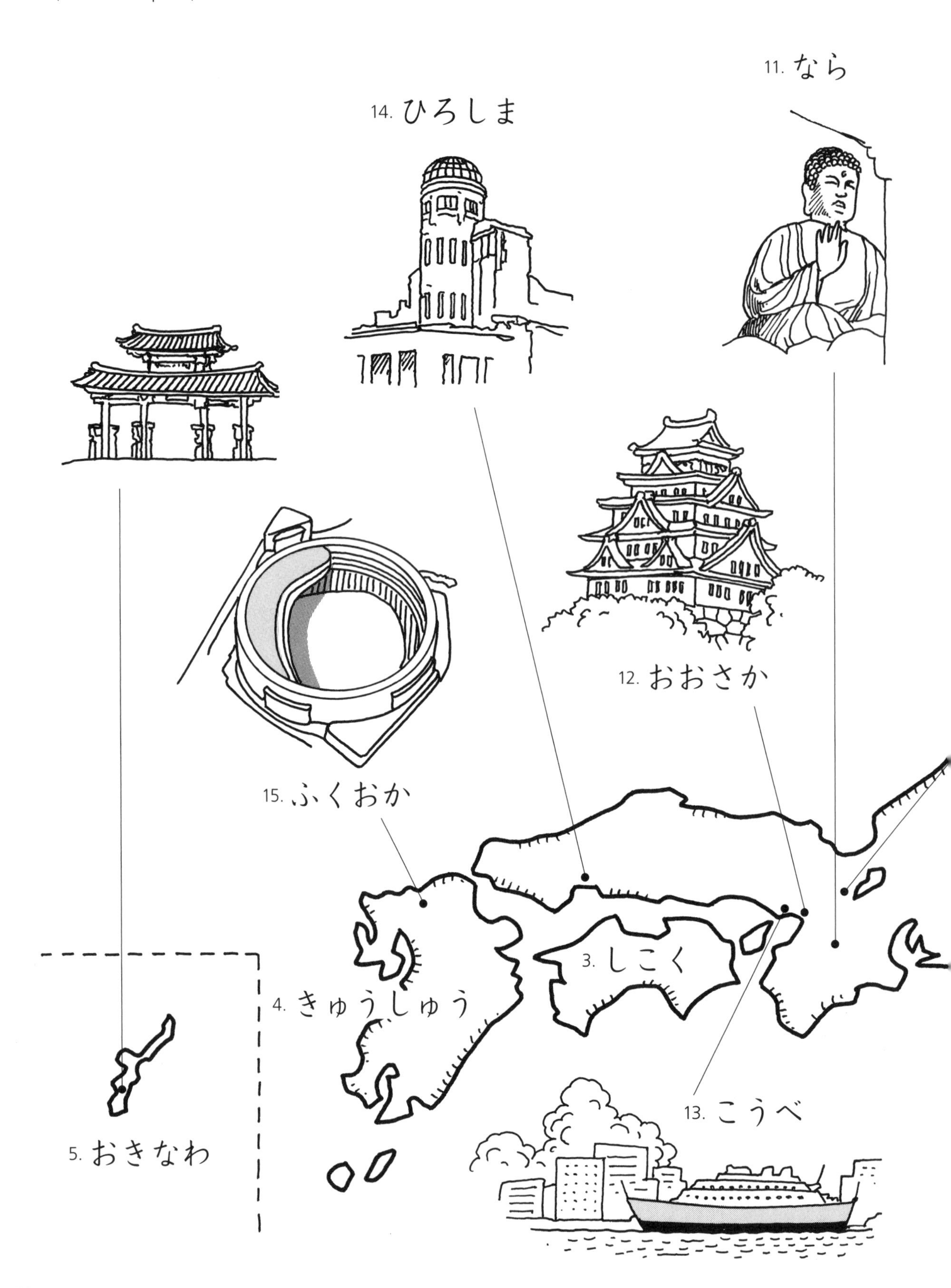

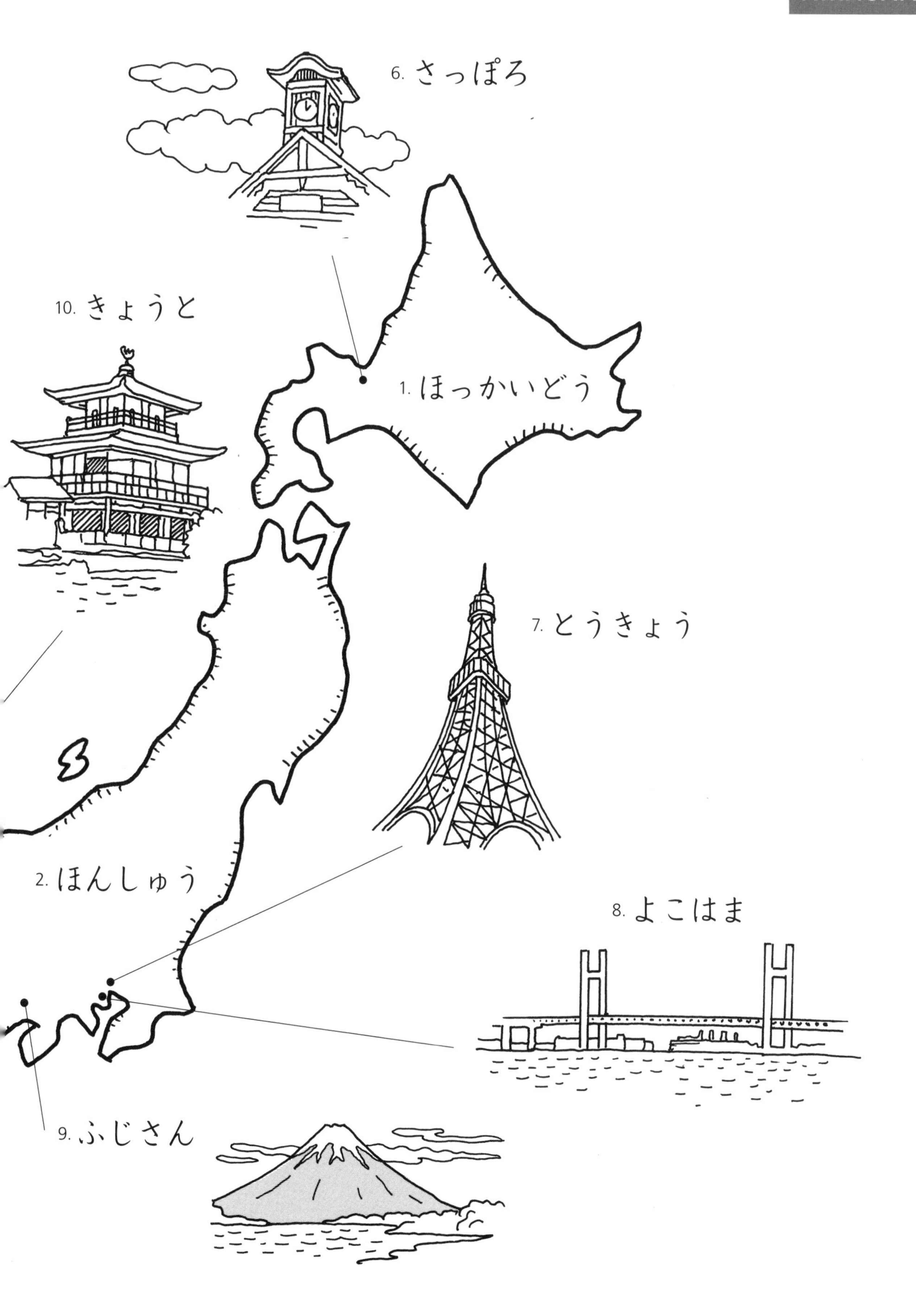
6. さっぽろ
10. きょうと
1. ほっかいどう
7. とうきょう
2. ほんしゅう
8. よこはま
9. ふじさん

READING CHALLENGE 2: Tokyo

(answers on p. 85)

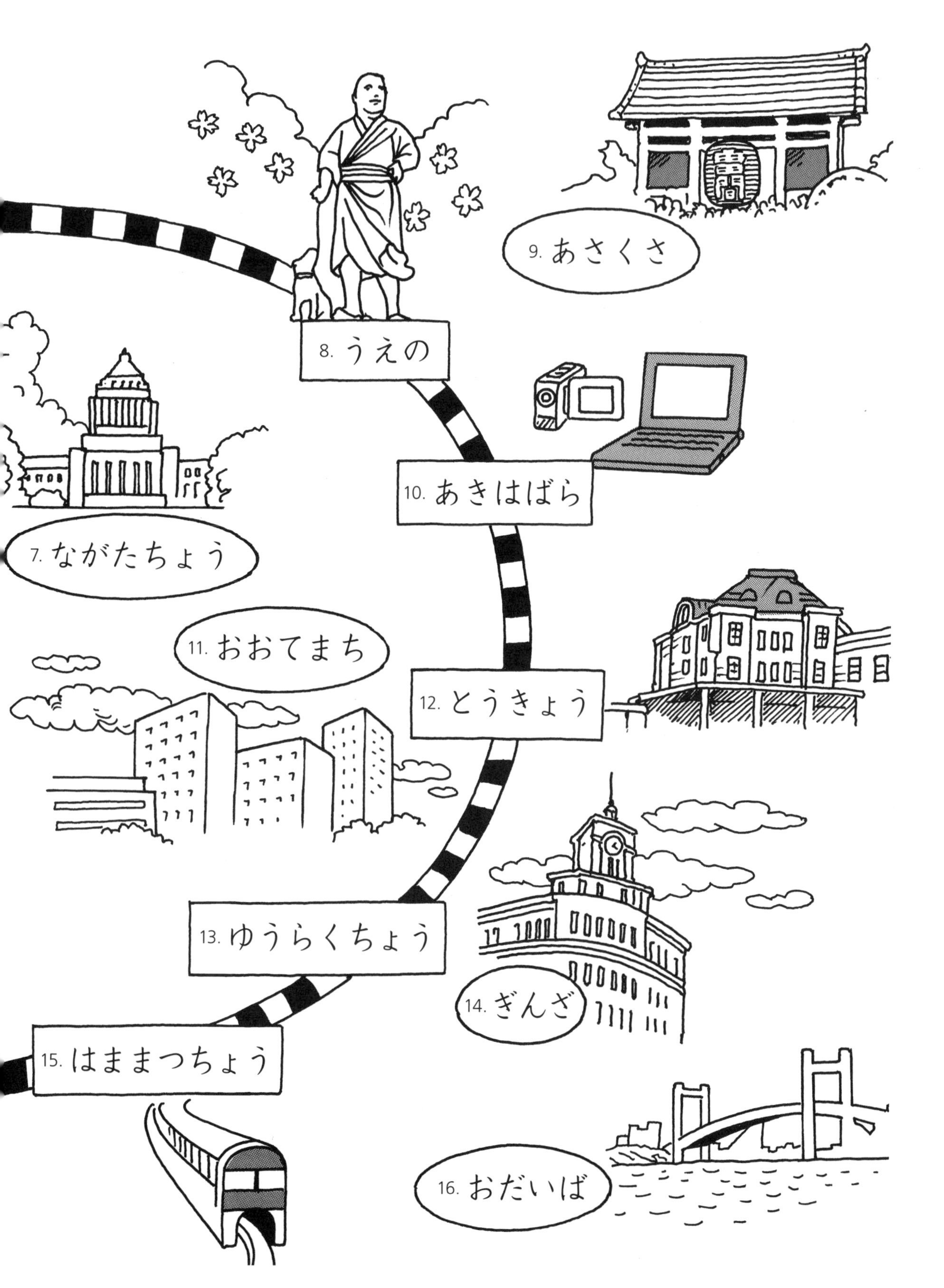

9. あさくさ
8. うえの
10. あきはばら
7. ながたちょう
11. おおてまち
12. とうきょう
13. ゆうらくちょう
14. ぎんざ
15. はままつちょう
16. おだいば

READING CHALLENGE 3: Japanese Food

(answers on p. 85)

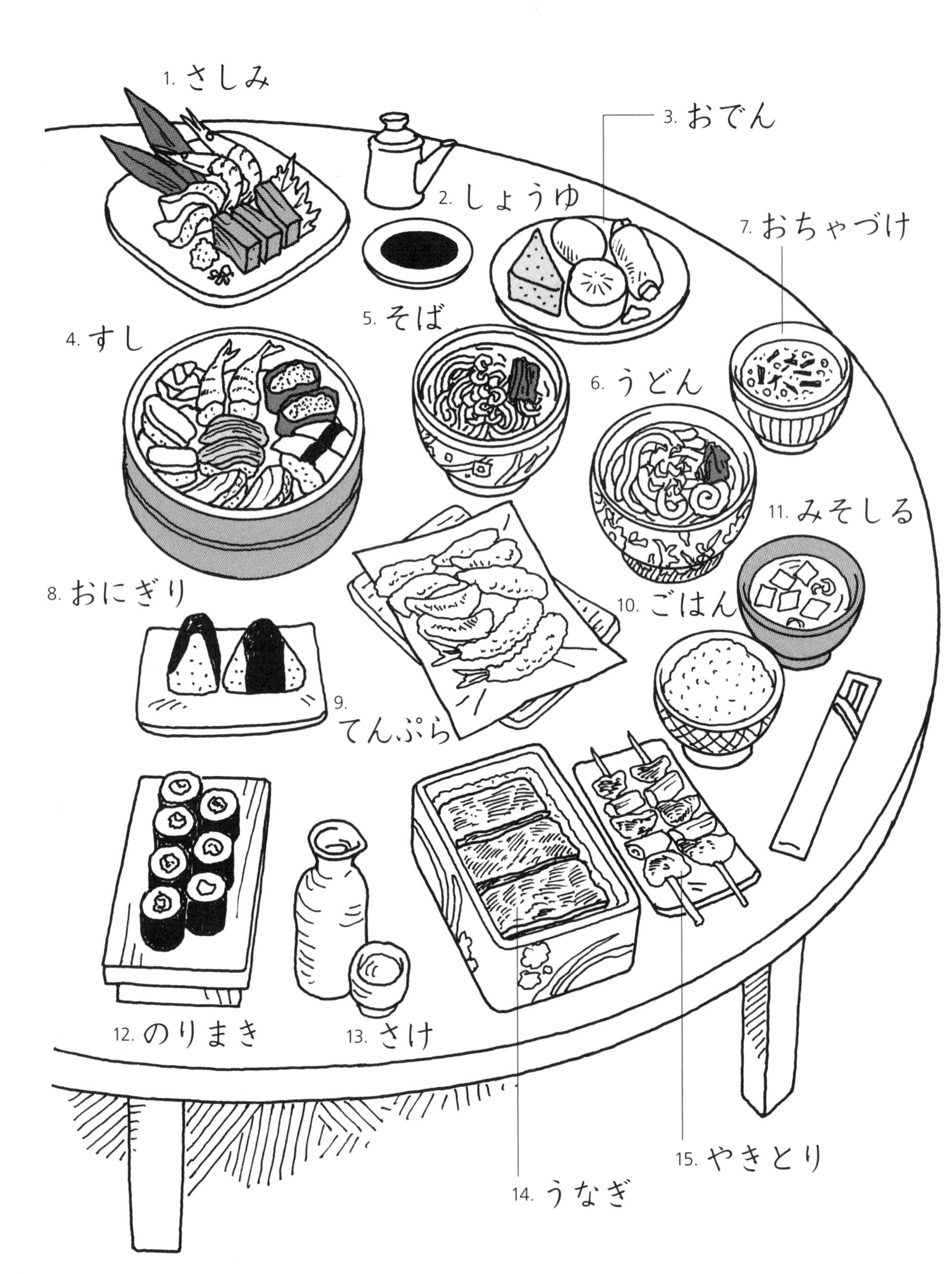

16. しゃぶしゃぶ
17. すきやき

READING CHALLENGE 4: A Japanese-style Room

(answers on pp. 85–86)

8. とこのま
9. かけじく
10. つぼ
11. しょうじ
12. ゆき
13. ものおき
14. にわ
15. ほうき

READING CHALLENGE 5: Daily Expressions (answers on p. 86)

Note: Japanese uses a (。) for a period, and a (、) for a comma.

1. おはようございます。

2. おやすみなさい。

3. いただきます。

4. ごちそうさまでした。

5. おめでとうございます。

6. どうも　ありがとうございます。

7. どういたしまして。

8. いってきます。

9. いってらっしゃい。

10. ただいま。

11. おかえりなさい。

12. おげんきですか。
    はい、げんきです。

Writing

Practice writing greeting cards.

1.

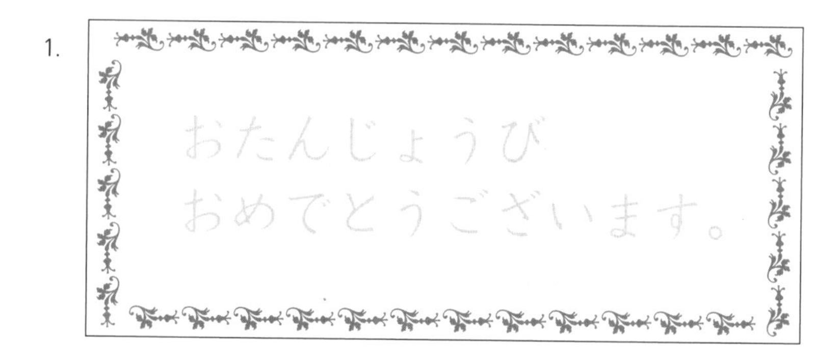

2.

いつも　いろいろ
ありがとうございます。

3.

あけまして
おめでとうございます。

ことしも　どうぞ　よろしく
おねがいします。

20XX. 1. 1

---

1. **O-tanjōbi omedetō gozaimasu.** (Happy birthday) 2. **Itsumo iroiro arigatō gozaimasu.** (Thank you for your constant kindness.) 3. **Akemashite omedetō gozaimasu.** (Happy New Year) **Kotoshi mo dōzo yoroshiku onegaishimasu** (I hope this year will be another good one for us. [lit. "I ask for you good will this year, too."])

は IS NOT ALWAYS *HA*

1. こんにちは。
Konnichiwa.
Good afternoon.

2. こんばんは。
Kombanwa.
Good evening.

Note that the particle *wa* is written は, not わ. When reading aloud, pause slightly after particles.

3. これは　ほんです。 **Kore wa hon desu.** This is a book.

4. それは　はなです。 **Sore wa hana desu.** That is a flower.

5. あれは　かさです。 **Are wa kasa desu.** That over there is an umbrella.

6. あれは　ぎんこうです。 **Are wa ginkō desu.** That is a bank.

7. わたしは　ささきです。 **Watashi wa Sasaki desu.** I am Sasaki.

8. ささきさんは　にほんじんです。 **Sasaki-san wa Nihon-jin desu.** Ms. Sasaki is a Japanese.

9. これは　ほんではありません。 **Kore wa hon dewa arimasen.** This is not a book.

10. それは　きってではありません。 **Sore wa kitte dewa arimasen.** That is not a stamp.

11. あれは　くるまではありません。 **Are wa kuruma dewa arimasen.** That over there is not a car.

へ IS NOT ALWAYS *E*

Note that the particle *e* is written へ.

1. かいしゃへ　いきます。

Kaisha e ikimasu.
I will go to the company.

2. うちへ　かえります。

Uchi e kaerimasu.
I will return home.

3. ともだちは　にほんへ　きます。

Tomodachi wa nihon e kimasu.
My friend will come to Japan.

4. くにへ　かえります。

Kuni e kaerimasu.
I will return to my country.

WHAT IS THE DIFFERENCE BETWEEN お AND を ?

The particle *o* is written を, not お. Keep in mind that を is never used to write any word in modern Japanese other than the particle を.

1. おちゃを　ください。

O-cha o kudasai.
I'll have green tea.

2. きってを　ください。

Kitte o kudasai.
Give me a stamp.

3. それを　みせてください。

Sore o misete kudasai.
Please show me that.

4. すしを　たべます。

Sushi o tabemasu.
I will eat sushi.

5. おさけを　のみます。

O-sake o nomimasu.
I will drink sake.

6. しんぶんを　よみます。

Shimbun o yomimasu.
I will read the newspaper.

7. べんきょうを　します。

Benkyō o shimasu.
I will study.

KATAKANA

BASIC SYLLABLES

Recognition of Forms

Some katakana look like their hiragana counterparts. Try to guess the readings of the following characters based on their similarities to characters you have already seen.

1. ウ
2. カ
3. キ
4. コ
5. セ
6. ヘ
7. モ
8. ヤ
9. ラ
10. リ
11. ナ
12. ニ
13. ヌ
14. ノ
15. メ
16. レ
17. シ
18. ツ
19. ソ
20. ン

---

1. **u** 2. **ka** 3. **ki** 4. **ko** 5. **se** 6. **he** 7. **mo** 8. **ya** 9. **ra** 10. **ri** 11. **na** 12. **ni** 13. **nu** 14. **no** 15. **me** 16. **re** 17. **shi** 18. **tsu** 19. **so** 20. **n**

Katakana Chart

ア あ a	イ い i	ウ う u	エ え e	オ お o
カ か ka	キ き ki	ク く ku	ケ け ke	コ こ ko
サ さ sa	シ し shi	ス す su	セ せ se	ソ そ so
タ た ta	チ ち chi	ツ つ tsu	テ て te	ト と to
ナ な na	ニ に ni	ヌ ぬ nu	ネ ね ne	ノ の no
ハ は ha	ヒ ひ hi	フ ふ fu	ヘ へ he	ホ ほ ho
マ ま ma	ミ み mi	ム む mu	メ め me	モ も mo
ヤ や ya		ユ ゆ yu		ヨ よ yo
ラ ら ra	リ り ri	ル る ru	レ れ re	ロ ろ ro
ワ わ wa				ヲ を o
ン ん n				

ガ が ga	ギ ぎ gi	グ ぐ gu	ゲ げ ge	ゴ ご go
ザ ざ za	ジ じ ji	ズ ず zu	ゼ ぜ ze	ゾ ぞ zo
ダ だ da	ヂ ぢ ji	ヅ づ zu	デ で de	ド ど do

バ ば ba	ビ び bi	ブ ぶ bu	ベ べ be	ボ ぼ bo
パ ぱ pa	ピ ぴ pi	プ ぷ pu	ペ ぺ pe	ポ ぽ po

Writing

The gray lines are aids to accurate style. As with hiragana, in writing katakana, the stroke order is from top to bottom, and from left to right.

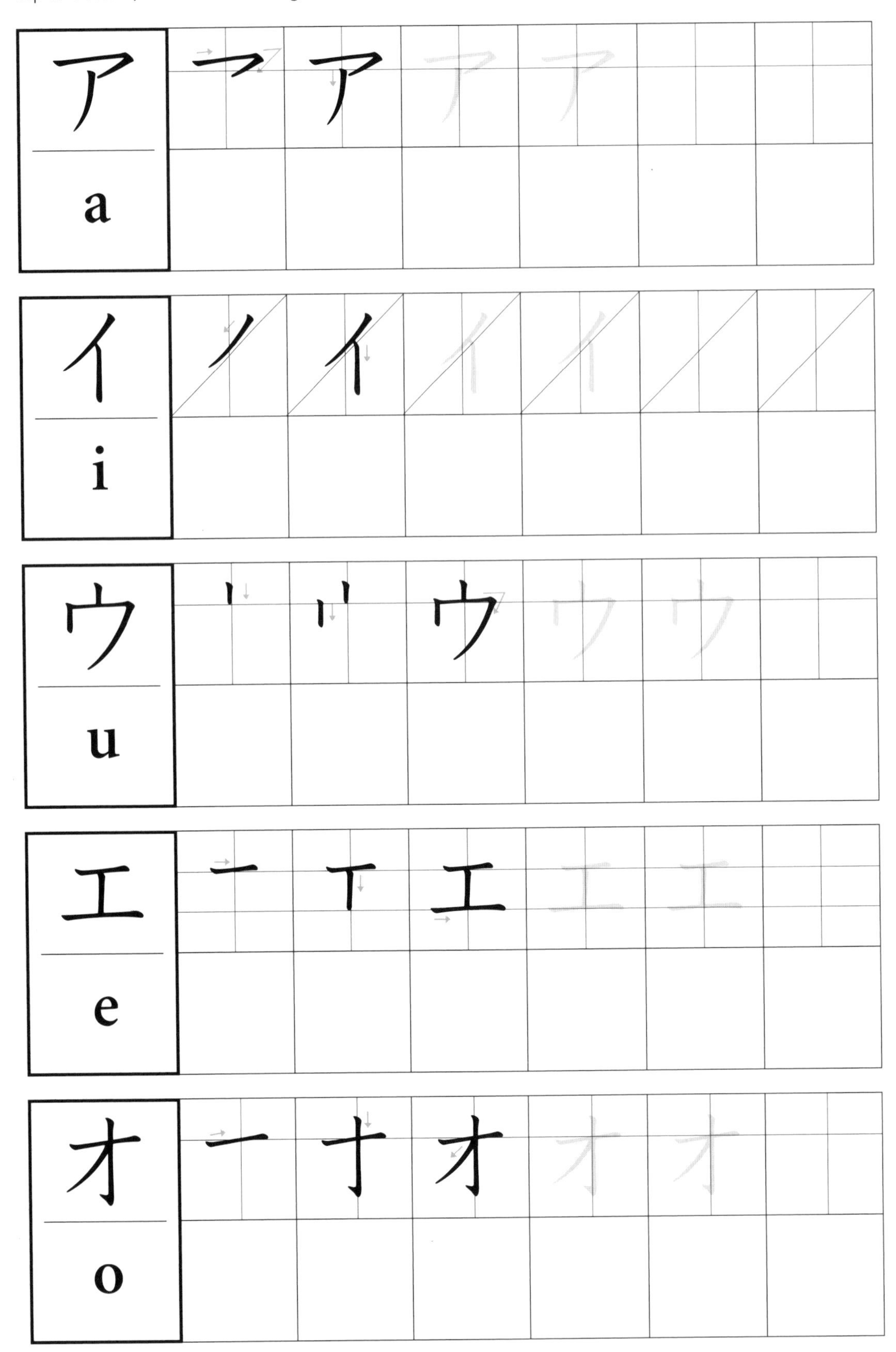

カ ka	フ	カ	カ	カ		
キ ki	一	二	キ	キ	キ	
ク ku	ノ	ク	ク	ク		
ケ ke	ノ	ｹ	ケ	ケ	ケ	
コ ko	フ	コ	コ	コ		

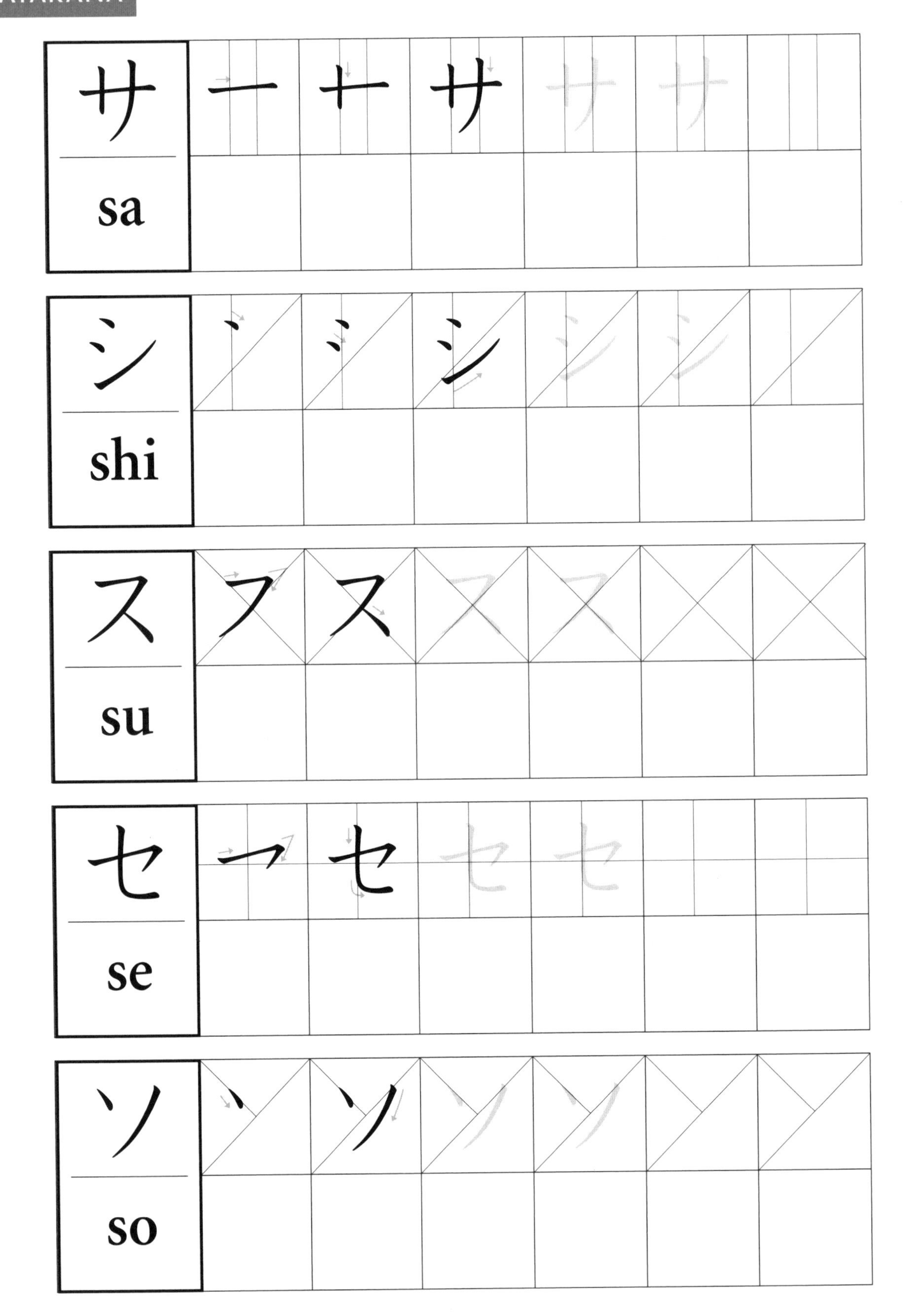
サ
sa
シ
shi
ス
su
セ
se
ソ
so

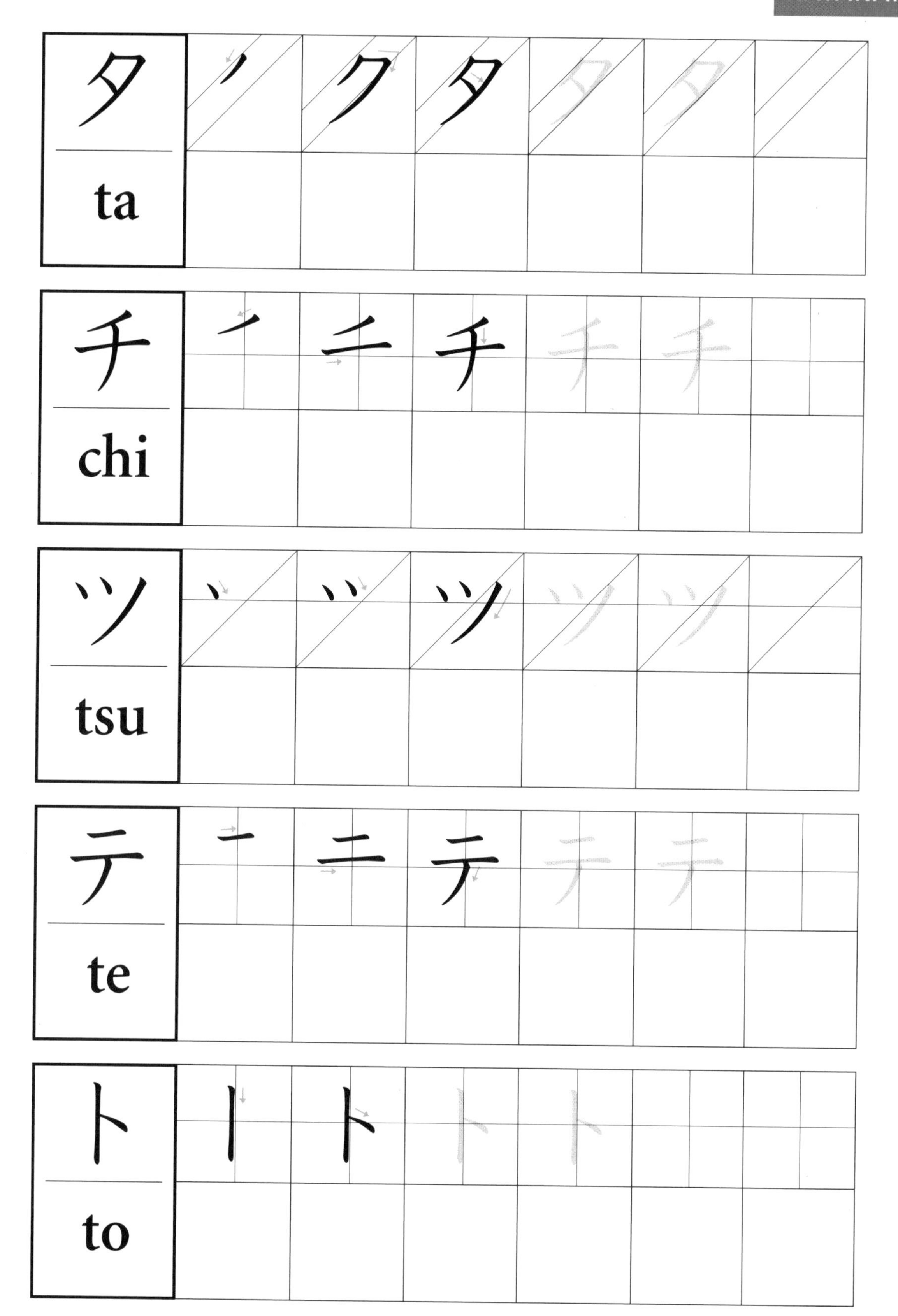
タ
ta
チ
chi
ツ
tsu
テ
te
ト
to

ナ na	ー	ナ	ナ	ナ		
ニ ni	ー	ニ	ニ	ニ		
ヌ nu	フ	ヌ	ヌ	ヌ		
ネ ne	丶	ラ	ネ	ネ	ネ	ネ
ノ no	ノ	ノ	ノ			

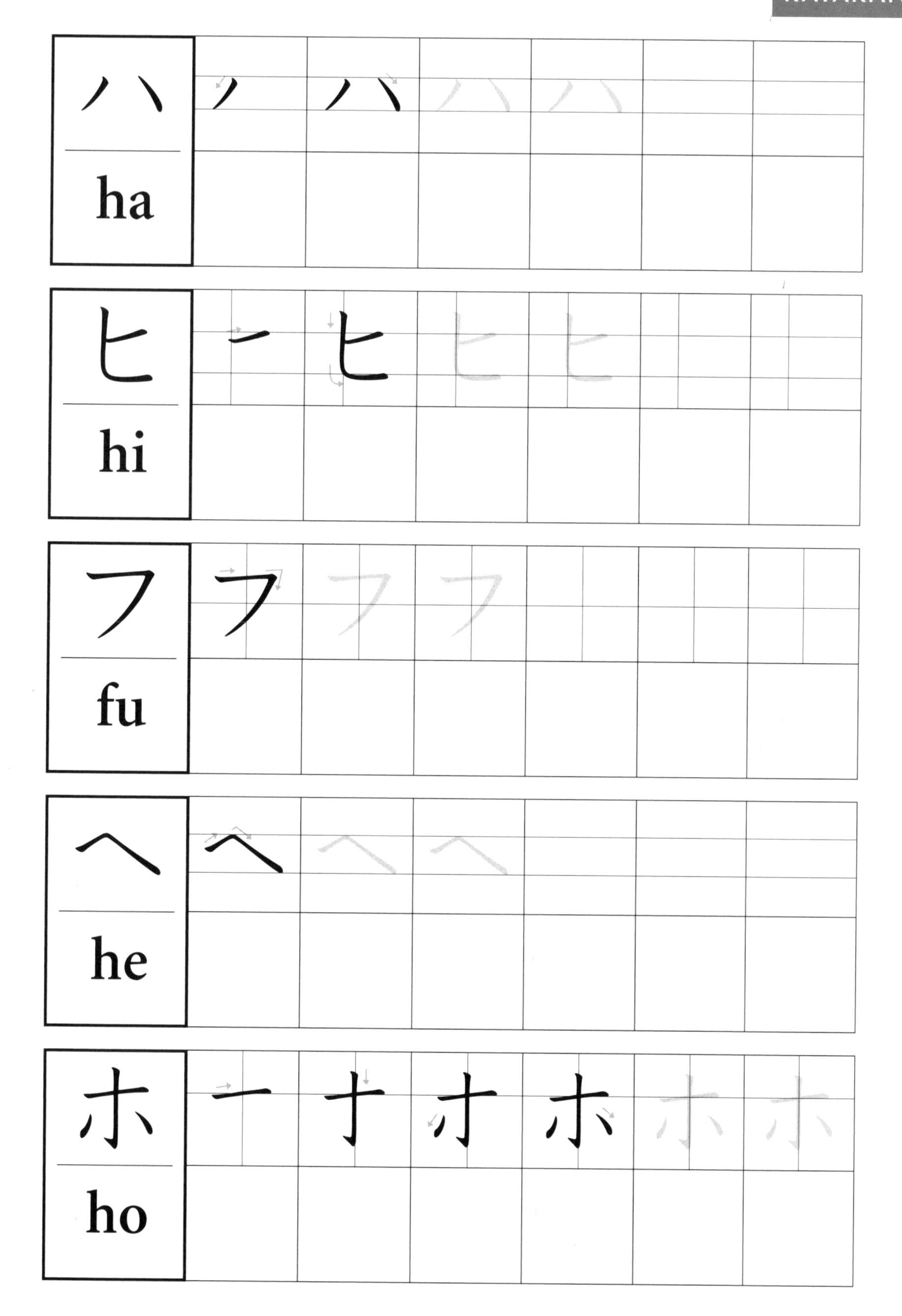
ハ
ha
ヒ
hi
フ
fu
ヘ
he
ホ
ho

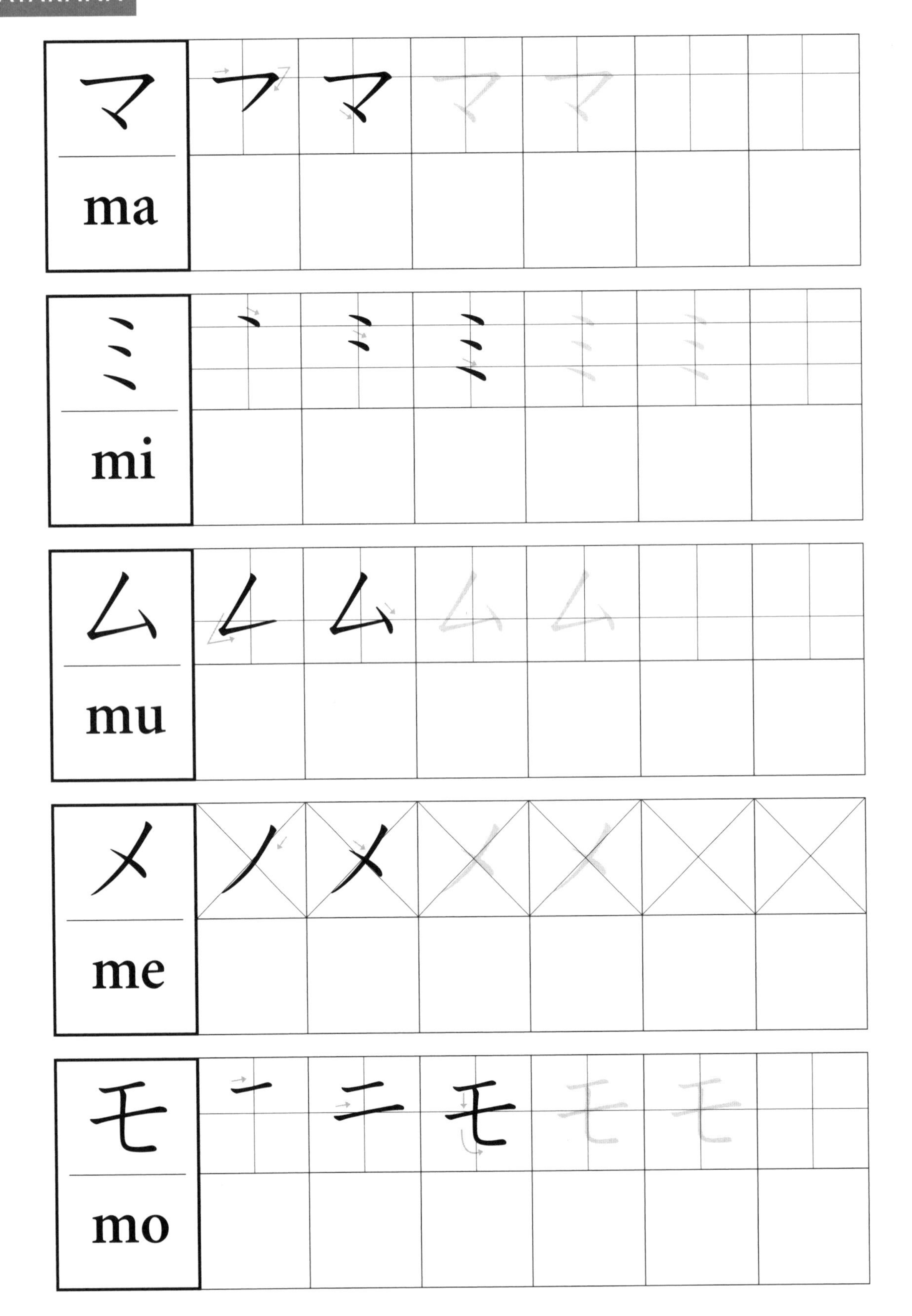
マ
ma
ミ
mi
ム
mu
メ
me
モ
mo

ヤ ya	ヤ	ヤ	ヤ	ヤ		
ユ yu	ユ	ユ	ユ	ユ		
ヨ yo	ヨ	ヨ	ヨ	ヨ	ヨ	

ラ ra						
リ ri						
ル ru						
レ re						
ロ ro						

ワ	ワ	ワ	ワ	ワ		
wa						

ヲ	ヲ	ヲ	ヲ	ヲ	ヲ	
o						

ン	ン	ン	ン	ン		
n						

VOICED & SEMIVOICED SYLLABLES

The (゛) and (゜) in ガ, パ, etc., should be written in the upper right-hand corner of the syllable. Write the following katakana, following the examples.

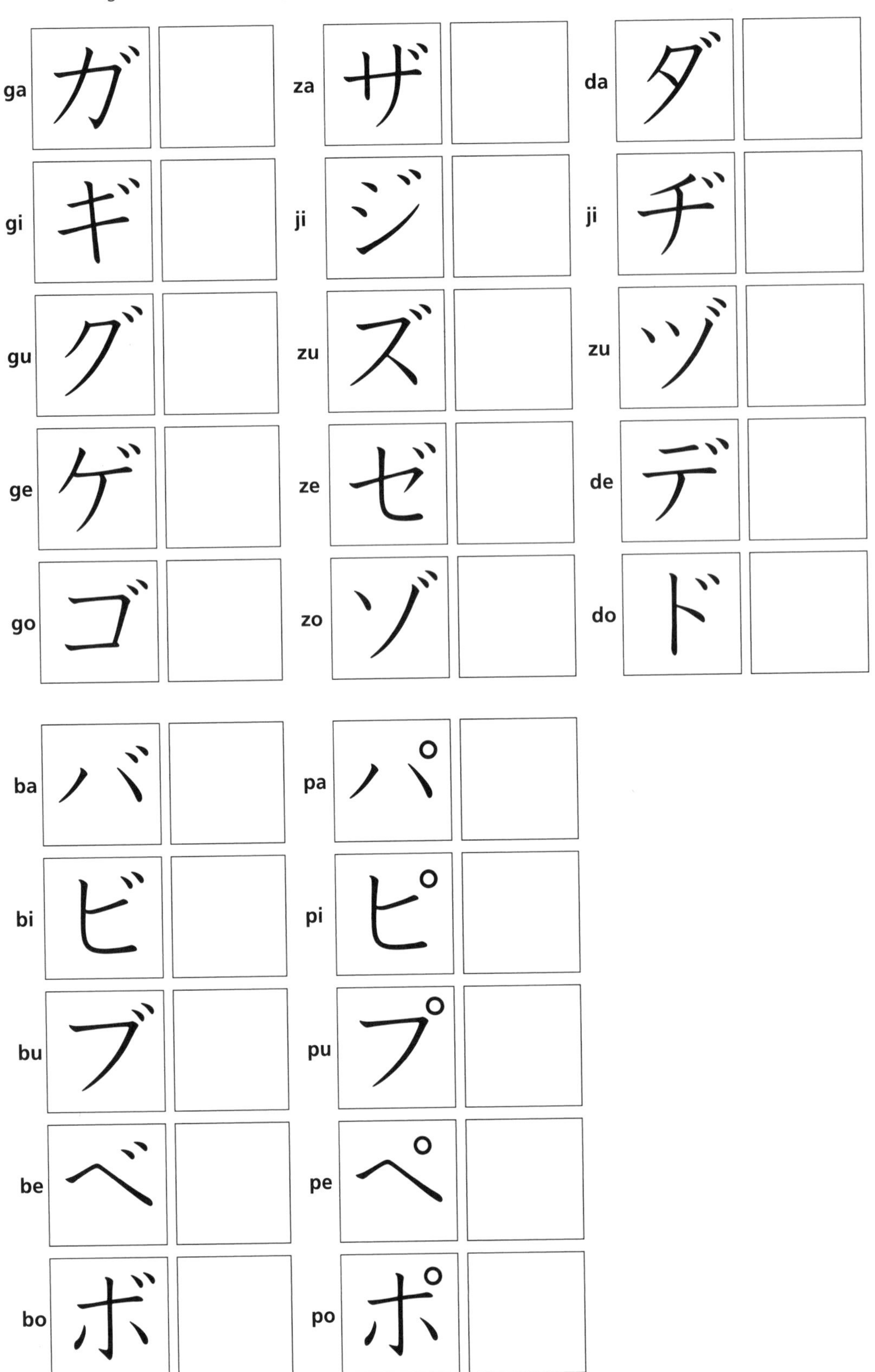

Reading & Writing

First read the words, then write them.

1. バス
2. ペン
3. カメラ
4. ゴルフ
5. ワイン
6. タオル
7. ピアノ
8. ビデオ
9. サンプル
10. カタログ
11. フロント
12. ドライブ

---

1. **basu** (bus) 2. **pen** (pen) 3. **kamera** (camera) 4. **gorufu** (golf) 5. **wain** (wine) 6. **taoru** (towel) 7. **piano** (piano) 8. **bideo** (video) 9. **sampuru** (sample) 10. **katarogu** (catalogue) 11. **furonto** (front desk) 12. **doraibu** (driving)

LOOK-ALIKE KATAKANA

The following pairs consist of look-alike syllables. Read, write, and distinguish them.

1. シ ツ
2. ウ ワ
3. サ ナ
4. ア ム 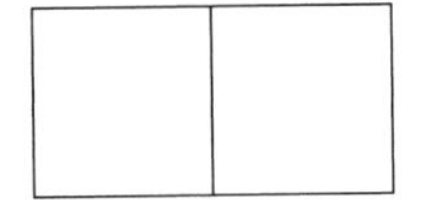
5. ワ フ
6. ニ ミ
7. ノ ハ 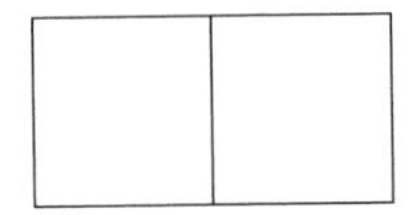
8. イ ト 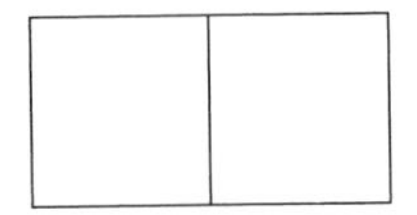
9. ク タ
10. ヒ エ 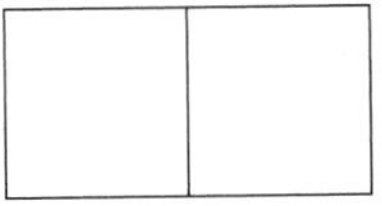
11. マ ム
12. オ ホ
13. ヌ ス 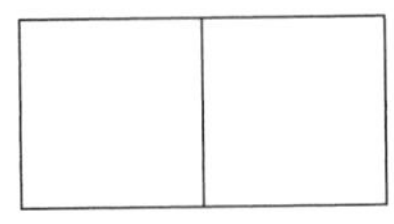
14. メ ナ
15. ル レ
16. ソ ン 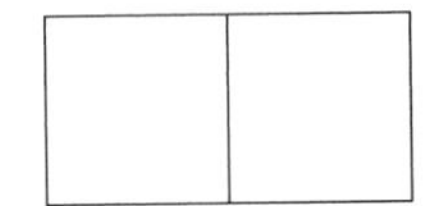
17. ヨ コ 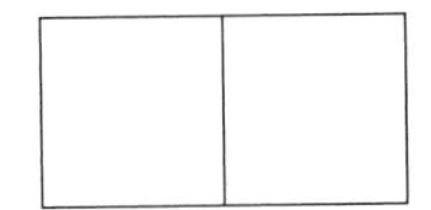
18. チ テ 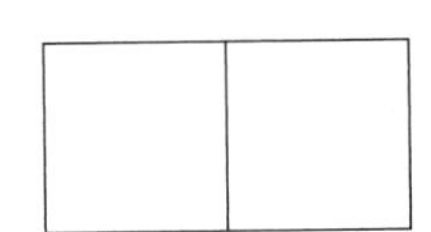

---

1. **shi tsu** 2. **u wa** 3. **sa na** 4. **a mu** 5. **wa fu** 6. **ni mi** 7. **no ha** 8. **i to** 9. **ku ta** 10. **hi e** 11. **ma mu** 12. **o ho** 13. **nu su** 14. **me na** 15. **ru re** 16. **so n** 17. **yo ko** 18. **chi te**

MODIFIED SYLLABLES

Recognition of Forms

As with hiragana, a consonant plus a small ャ, ュ, or ョ is pronounced as a single syllable.

キャ キュ キョ　　ギャ ギュ ギョ

kya kyu kyo　　gya gyu gyo

シャ シュ ショ　　ジャ ジュ ジョ

sha shu sho　　ja ju jo

チャ チュ チョ

cha chu cho

ニャ ニュ ニョ

nya nyu nyo

ヒャ ヒュ ヒョ　　ビャ ビュ ビョ　　ピャ ピュ ピョ

hya hyu hyo　　bya byu byo　　pya pyu pyo

ミャ ミュ ミョ

mya myu myo

リャ リュ リョ

rya ryu ryo

Reading & Writing

In katakana, too, small ャ, ュ, and ョ are written about one-fourth the size of a normal character.

1. シャツ
2. ジャズ
3. キャベツ
4. チャンス
5. ジャンル
6. マンション
7. ジョギング
8. キャンセル

1. **shatsu** (shirts) 2. **jazu** (jazz) 3. **kyabetsu** (cabbage) 4. **chansu** (chance) 5. **janru** (genre) 6. **manshon** (apartment, condominium) 7. **jogingu** (jogging) 8. **kyanseru** (cancel)

DOUBLE CONSONANTS

Reading & Writing

The double consonants *kk*, *ss*, *tt*, and *pp* are indicated in katakana with a small ッ.

1. カップ
2. バッグ
3. ラケット
4. キッチン
5. ネックレス
6. サンドイッチ
7. パンフレット
8. ピックアップ

1. **kappu** (cup) 2. **baggu** (bag) 3. **raketto** (racket) 4. **kitchin** (kitchen) 5. **nekkuresu** (necklace) 6. **sandoitchi** (sandwich) 7. **panfuretto** (pamphlet) 8. **pikkuappu** (pickup)

LONG VOWELS

Reading & Writing

In katakana, long sounds are represented by a dash 一.

1. スキー
2. プール
3. ゲーム
4. デパート
5. セーター
6. レポート
7. ハンバーガー
8. メールアドレス
9. スポーツクラブ

1. **sukī** (skiing) 2. **pūru** (pool) 3. **gēmu** (game) 4. **depāto** (department store) 5. **sēta** (sweater) 6. **repōto** (report) 7. **hambāgā** (hamburger) 8. **mēru-adoresu** (mail address) 9. **supōtsu-kurabu** (gym, fitness club)

COMBINATION OF MODIFIED AND OTHER SYLLABLES

Reading & Writing

1. ジュース

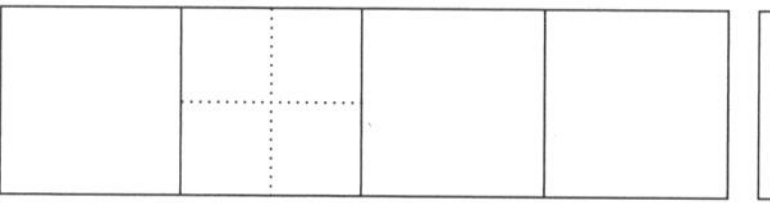
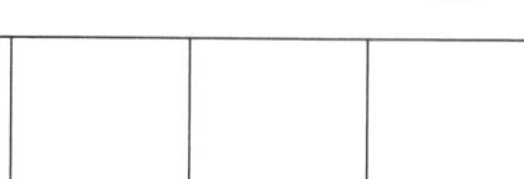

2. メニュー

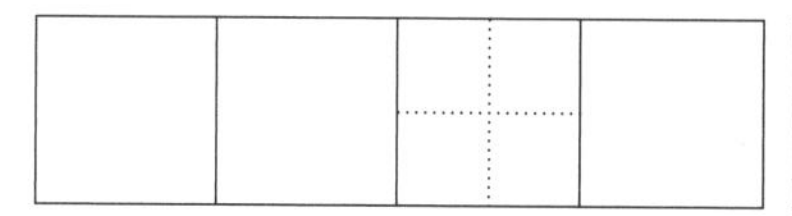
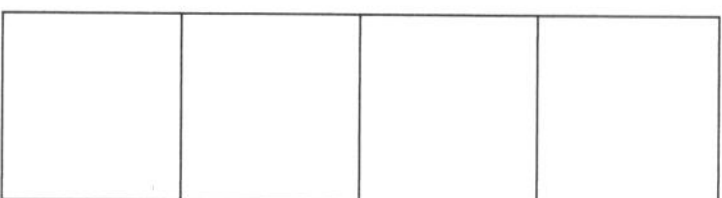

3. ギャップ

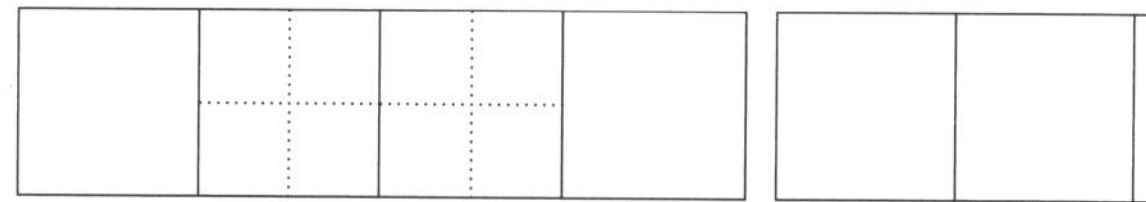

4. フラッシュ

5. コンピューター

6. ミュージカル

7. ショッピング

8. シャープペンシル

---

1. **jūsu** (juice) 2. **menyū** (menu) 3. **gappu** (gap) 4. **furasshu** (flash) 5. **kompyūtā** (computer)
6. **myūjikaru** (musical) 7. **shoppingu** (shopping) 8. **shāpu-penshiru** (mechanical pencil)

VERTICAL LAYOUT

The same rules that apply to writing hiragana vertically apply to katakana. Note, however, that ー is also written vertically.

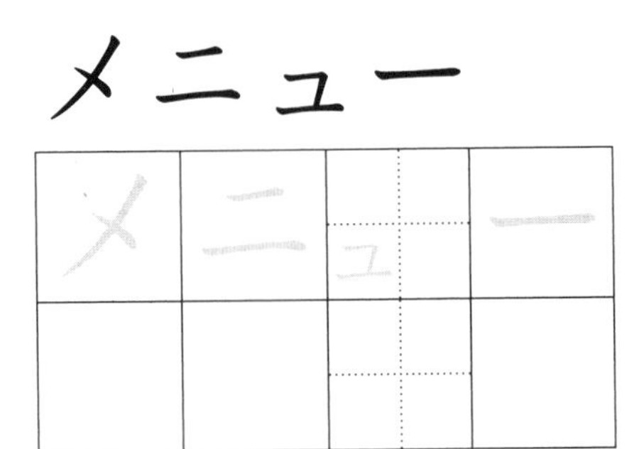

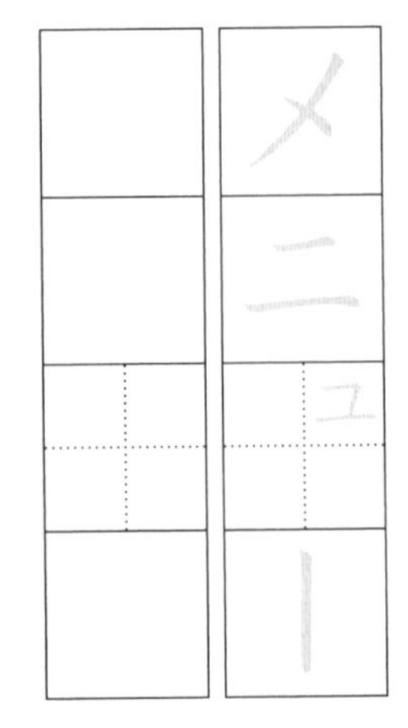

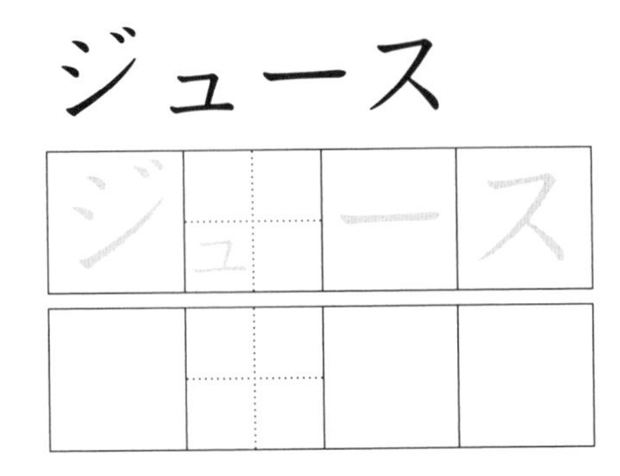

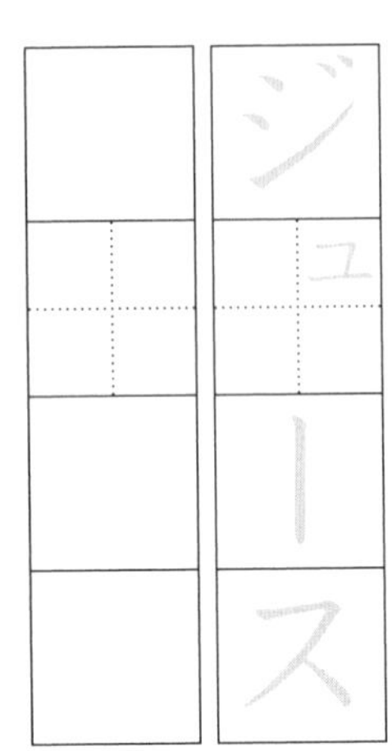

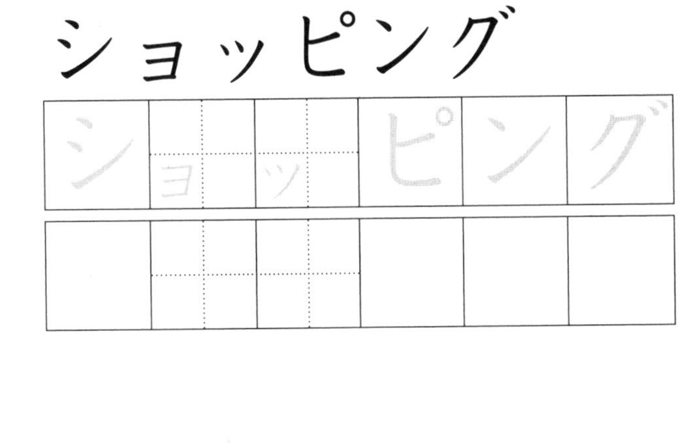

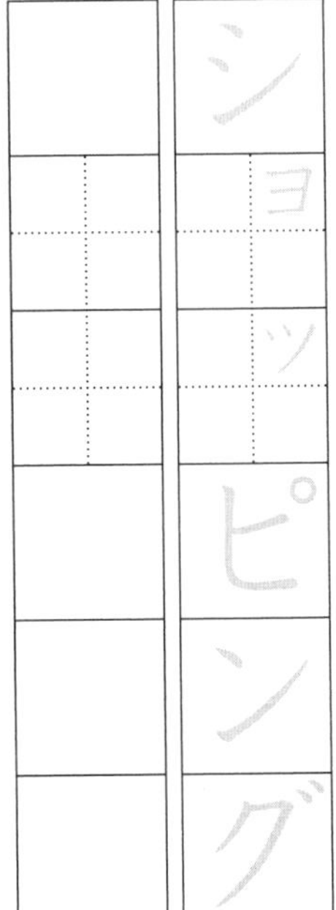

HOW TO READ LOANWORDS

Japanese is rife with words borrowed from other languages. Read the following words borrowed from English and try guessing their meanings based on how they sound.

1. ファイル

The small vowels ァ, ィ, ゥ, ェ, and ォ should be read together with the character that comes before them. For example, ファ is not *fua* but *fa*, and フィ is not *fui* but *fi*. These character-and-small-vowel combinations are all one syllable in length, just like the other modified vowels you have learned.

2. オフィス
3. フュージョン
4. フェア
5. フォーム
6. パーティー
7. チェック
8. ハードディスク
9. ヴィーナス

ヴ is used to express the consonant "v." The modified syllables beginning with this kana are ヴァ *va*, ヴィ *vi*, ヴェ *ve*, and ヴォ *vo*.

10. ヴォーカル

---

1. **fairu** (file) 2. **ofisu** (office) 3. **fyūjon** (fusion) 4. **fea** (fair) 5. **fōmu** (form) 6. **pātī** (party) 7. **chekku** (check) 8. **hādodisuku** (hard disk) 9. **Vīnasu** (Venus) 10. **vōkaru** (vocal)

READING CHALLENGE 1: The World

(answers on p. 86)

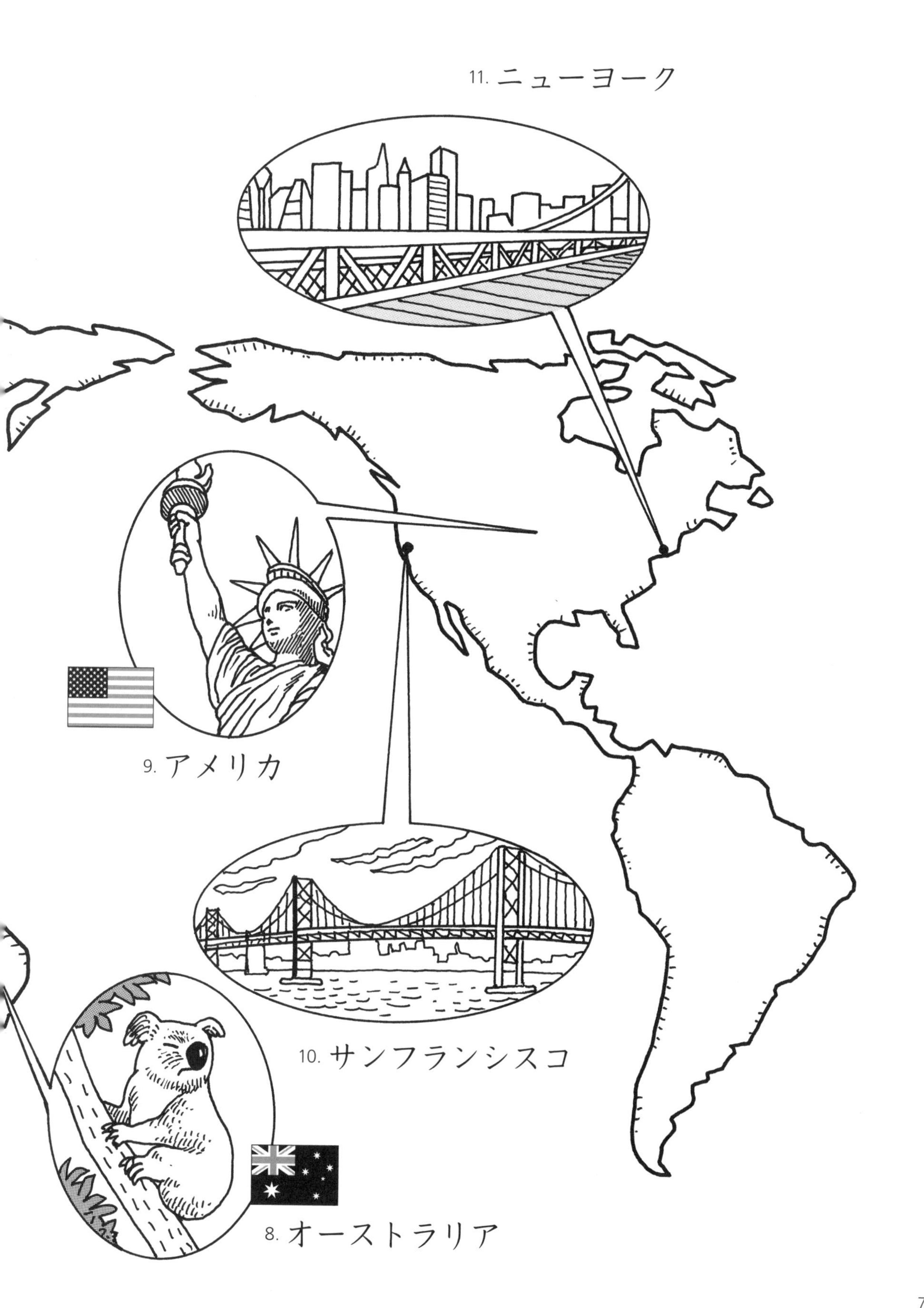
11. ニューヨーク
9. アメリカ
10. サンフランシスコ
8. オーストラリア

READING CHALLENGE 2: At a Party

TRACK 28

(answers on pp. 86–87)

8. ネクタイ
9. ワイシャツ
10. ジャケット
11. スーツ
12. ベルト
13. ズボン
26. ウイスキー
27. ビール
BEER
28. ワイン
29. コーヒー
30. ミルク
31. ジュース
ジュース
32. コーラ
33. グラス

READING CHALLENGE 3: A Western-style Room

TRACK 29

(answers on p. 87)

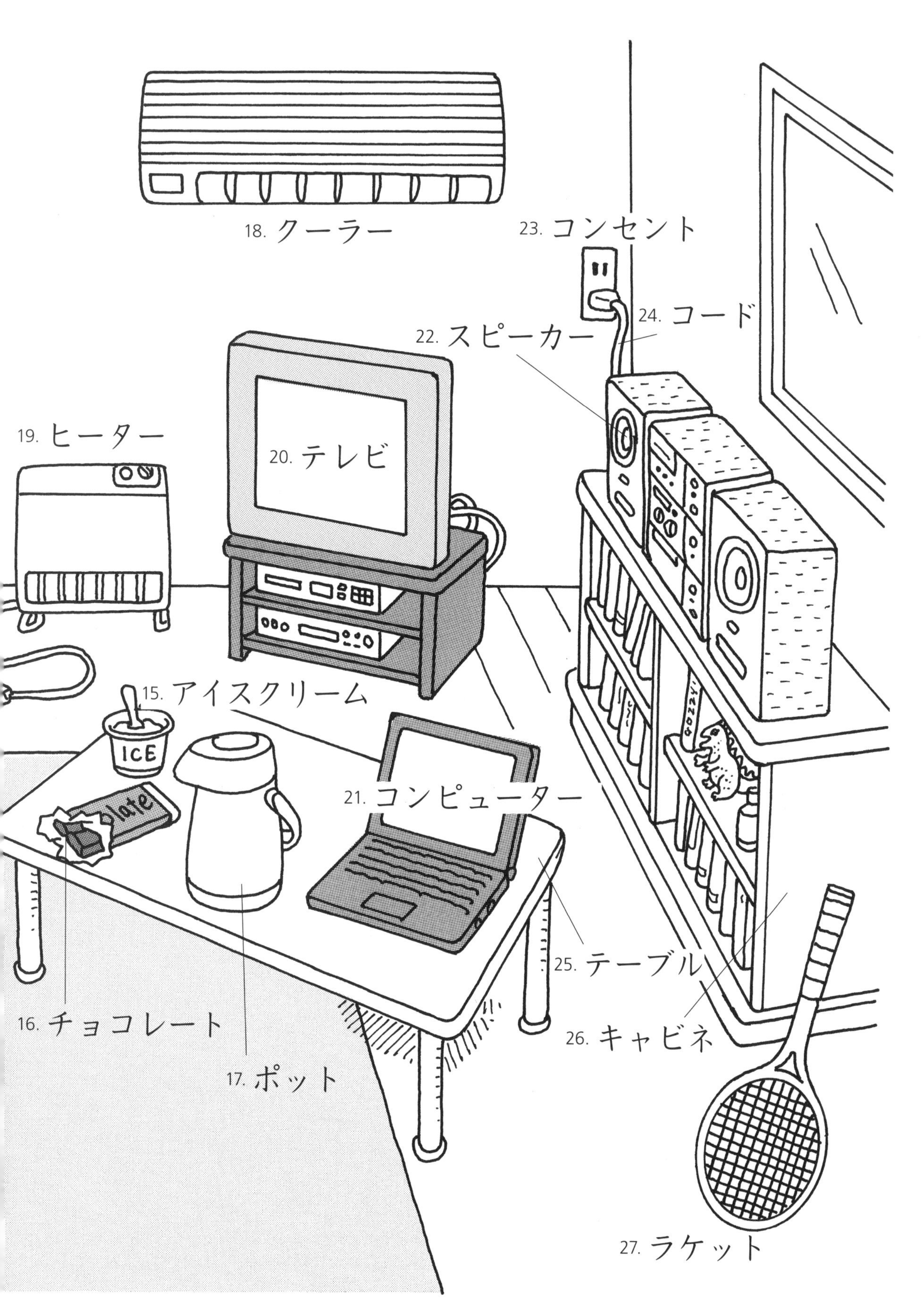
18. クーラー
23. コンセント
24. コード
22. スピーカー
19. ヒーター
20. テレビ
15. アイスクリーム
ICE
late
21. コンピューター
25. テーブル
16. チョコレート
26. キャビネ
17. ポット
27. ラケット

ONOMATOPOEIA

Japanese uses an abundance of onomatopoeic words, some that mimic sounds and some that mimic states. Read the words below and try to guess their meanings.

1. ニャーニャー

2. ワンワン

3. コケコッコー

4. ゴロゴロ

5. ザーザー

6. トントン

---

1. **nyā-nyā** (meow) 2. **wan-wan** (bow-wow) 3. **kokekokkō** (cock-a-doodle-doo) 4. **goro-goro** (sound of thunder) 5. **zā-zā** (sound of heavy rain) 6. **ton-ton** (knock-knock)

SHORTENED WORDS

Many words of foreign origin that are long and tedious to pronounce in Japanese are shortened so that they are easier to say. Try guessing the meanings of these words:

1. リモコン
2. パソコン
3. エアコン
4. デジカメ
5. プレゼン
6. コンビニ
7. ファミレス
8. セレブ

---

1. **rimo-kon** (remote control) 2. **paso-kon** (personal computer) 3. **ea-kon** (air conditioner) 4. **deji-kame** (digital camera) 5. **pure-zen** (presentation) 6. **kombini** (convenience store) 7. **fami-resu** (family restaurant) 8. **serebu** (celebrity)

ENGLISH MADE IN JAPAN

There are also many words that sound like they have come from English but not quite, because they are not arranged or used in the English way. These are known as *wasei-Eigo* ("Japanese-manufactured English words") and they are purely Japanese inventions. Try guessing some:

1. チアガール
2. プッシュホン
3. グレードアップ
4. フライドポテト
5. リサイクルショップ
6. ベビーカー
7. モーニングサービス
8. ライブハウス
9. ジーパン
10. マイブーム

---

1. **chiagāru** ("cheer girl," cheerleader) 2. **pusshuhon** ("push phone," touch-tone phone) 3. **gurēdo-appu** ("grade-up," upgrade, improvement) 4. **furaidopoteto** ("fried potato," french fry) 5. **risaikuru-shoppu** ("recycle shop," second-hand shop) 6. **bebīkā** ("baby car," baby carriage) 7. **mōningusābisu** ("mornig service," breakfast special) 8. **raibuhausu** ("live house," club/bar offering live music) 9. **jīpan** ("jeans pants," jeans) 10. **maibūmu** ("my boom," what I'm really into these days)

WRITING CHALLENGE 1

Try writing the following English words in katakana, following the examples.

jam	→	ジ	ャ	ム	
sport(s)	→	ス	ポ	ー	ツ
lunch	→	ラ	ン	チ	
super	→	ス	ー	パ	ー

hotel	→	ホ	テ	ル
test	→	テ	ス	ト
match	→	マ	ッ	チ
top	→	ト	ッ	プ

1. model →
2. business →
3. pattern →
4. money →
5. rate →
6. maker →
7. user →
8. system →
9. message →
10. schedule →

1. モデル (**moderu**) 2. ビジネス (**bijinesu**) 3. パターン (**patān**) 4. マネー (**manē**) 5. レート (**rēto**) 6. メーカー (**mēkā**) 7. ユーザー (**yūzā**) 8. システム (**shisutemu**) 9. メッセージ (**messēji**) 10. スケジュール (**sukejūru**)

WRITING CHALLENGE 2

Try writing the words in Japanese, following the examples. Hint: There is only one right answer for each pair.

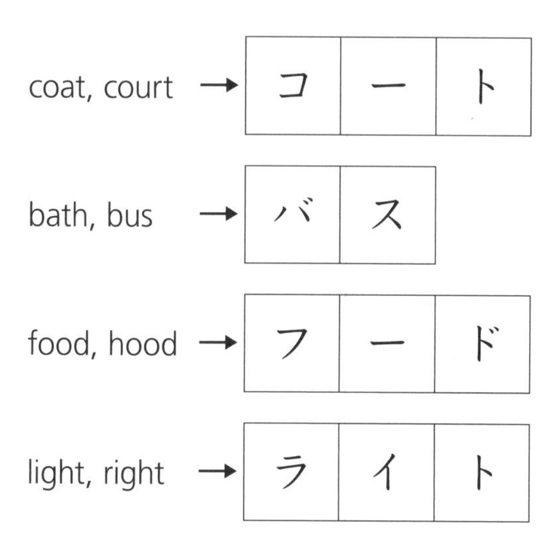

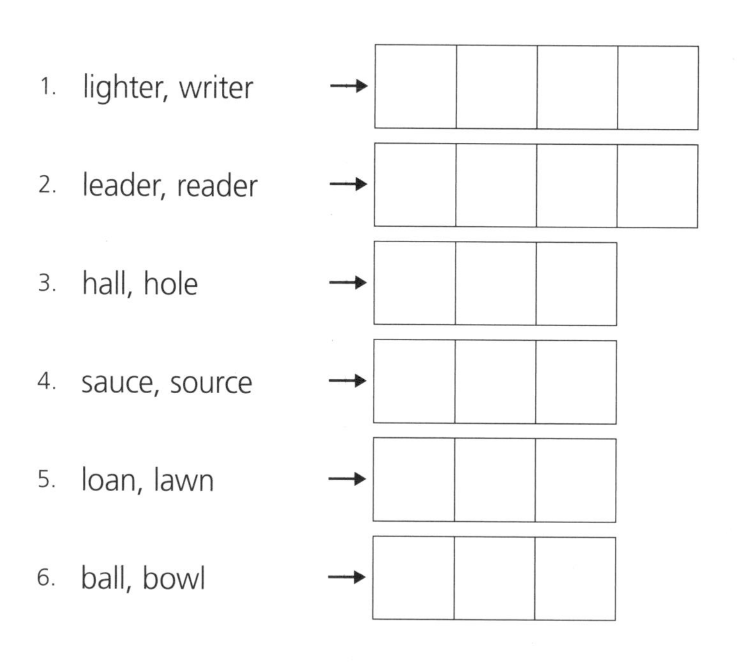

1. ライター (**raitā**) 2. リーダー (**rīda**) 3. ホール (**hōru**) 4. ソース (**sōsu**) 5. ローン (**rōn**) 6. ボール (**bōru**)

COMPREHENSIVE READING CHALLENGE

Try reading the following combinations of hiragana and katakana.

1. けしゴム
2. ドイツじん
3. フランスご
4. ロンドンぎんこう
5. バスのりば
6. タクシーのりば
7. パンや
8. ローマじ
9. なまビール
10. とうきょうタワー
11. これは　メールアドレスです。
12. それは　チケットです。
13. あれは　カメラです。
14. ビールを　ください。
15. サンドイッチと　コーヒーを　ください。

---

1. **keshigomu** (eraser) 2. **Doitsu-jin** (German person) 3. **Furansu-go** (French language) 4. **Rondon ginkō** (Bank of London) 5. **basu-noriba** (bus terminal) 6. **takushī-noriba** (taxi stand) 7. **pan-ya** (bakery) 8. **rōma-ji** (romanized Japanese) 9. **nama-bīru** (draft beer) 10. **Tōkyō-tawā** (Tokyo Tower) 11. **Kore wa mēru-adoresu desu.** (This is an e-mail address.) 12. **Sore wa chiketto desu.** (That is a ticket.) 13. **Are wa kamera desu**. (That over there is a camera.) 14. **Bīru o kudasai.** (Give me a beer.) 15. **Sandoitchi to kōhi o kudasai.** (Give me a sandwich and a coffee.)

ANSWERS TO READING CHALLENGES

HIRAGANA

READING CHALLENGE 1: Japan

1. ほっかいどう **Hokkaidō**
2. ほんしゅう **Honshū**
3. しこく **Shikoku**
4. きゅうしゅう **Kyūshū**
5. おきなわ **Okinawa**
6. さっぽろ **Sapporo**
7. とうきょう **Tōkyō**
8. よこはま **Yokohama**
9. ふじさん **Fujisan** Mt. Fuji
10. きょうと **Kyōto**
11. なら **Nara**
12. おおさか **Ōsaka**
13. こうべ **Kōbe**
14. ひろしま **Hiroshima**
15. ふくおか **Fukuoka**

READING CHALLENGE 2: Tokyo

1. いけぶくろ **Ikebukuro**
2. しんじゅく **Shinjuku**
3. しぶや **Shibuya**
4. ろっぽんぎ **Roppongi**
5. えびす **Ebisu**
6. しながわ **Shinagawa**
7. ながたちょう **Nagatachō**
8. うえの **Ueno**
9. あさくさ **Asakusa**
10. あきはばら **Akihabara**
11. おおてまち **Ōtemachi**
12. とうきょう **Tōkyō**
13. ゆうらくちょう **Yūrakuchō**
14. ぎんざ **Ginza**
15. はままつちょう **Hamamatsuchō**
16. おだいば **Odaiba**

READING CHALLENGE 3: Japanese Food

1. さしみ **sashimi** sashimi, raw fish
2. しょうゆ **shōyu** soy sauce
3. おでん **oden** one-pot "stew" consisting of boiled eggs, daikon, devil's tongue jelly, fish cakes, and other ingredients cooked in a soy-flavored broth
4. すし **sushi** sushi
5. そば **soba** buckwheat noodles
6. うどん **udon** wheat noodles
7. おちゃづけ **ochazuke** hot green tea over rice mixed with nori, shreds of salmon, umeboshi, and/or other ingredients
8. おにぎり **onigiri** rice ball
9. てんぷら **tempura** tempura
10. ごはん **gohan** rice
11. みそしる **misoshiru** miso soup
12. のりまき **norimaki** sushi roll
13. さけ **sake** sake
14. うなぎ **unagi** eel, broiled eel
15. やきとり **yakitori** barbecued chicken
16. しゃぶしゃぶ **shabushabu** shabu-shabu
17. すきやき **sukiyaki** sukiyaki

READING CHALLENGE 4: A Japanese-style Room

1. おしいれ **oshiire** closet
2. ふとん **futon** futon
3. ふすま **fusuma** sliding paper door
4. たたみ **tatami** tatami mat
5. ざぶとん **zabuton** cushion

6. こたつ **kotatsu** blanket-covered table heated underneath
7. みかん **mikan** tangerine, mandarin orange
8. とこのま **tokonoma** alcove
9. かけじく **kakejiku** scroll painting
10. つぼ **tsubo** vase
11. しょうじ **shōji** sliding paper partition
12. ゆき **yuki** snow
13. ものおき **mono-oki** shed
14. にわ **niwa** garden, yard
15. ほうき **hōki** broom

READING CHALLENGE 5: Daily Expressions

1. おはようございます。
   ohayō gozaimasu
   good morning
2. おやすみなさい。
   oyasuminasai
   good night
3. いただきます。
   itadakimasu
   lit., "I will partake" [said before eating]
4. ごちそうさまでした。
   gochisōsamadeshita
   "thanks for the meal" [said after finishing a meal]
5. おめでとうございます。
   omedetōgozaimasu
   congratulations
6. どうも　ありがとうございます。
   dōmo arigatō gozaimasu
   thank you very much
7. どういたしまして。
   dōitashimashite
   you are welcome
8. いってきます。
   ittekimasu
   so long [said when you are leaving the house]
9. いってらっしゃい。
   itterasshai
   so long [said to someone leaving the house]
10. ただいま。
    tadaima
    I'm home
11. おかえりなさい。
    okaerinasai
    welcome home
12. おげんきですか。
    o-genki desu ka
    how are you?
    はい、げんきです。
    hai, genki desu
    I'm fine

KATAKANA

READING CHALLENGE 1: The World

1. イギリス **Igirisu** United Kingdom
2. ロンドン **Rondon** London
3. フランス **Furansu** France
4. スイス **Suisu** Switzerland
5. イタリア **Itaria** Italy
6. ローマ **Rōma** Rome
7. タイ **Tai** Thailand
8. オーストラリア **Ōsutoraria** Australia
9. アメリカ **Amerika** United States
10. サンフランシスコ **Sanfuranshisuko** San Francisco
11. ニューヨーク **Nyūyōku** New York

READING CHALLENGE 2: At a Party

1. スカーフ **sukāfu** scarf
2. イヤリング **iyaringu** earring
3. ネックレス **nekkuresu** necklace
4. セーター **sētā** sweater
5. スカート **sukāto** skirt

6. ワンピース **wampīsu** dress
7. ハイヒール **haihīru** high heels
8. ネクタイ **nekutai** necktie
9. ワイシャツ **waishatsu** dress shirt
10. ジャケット **jaketto** sports coat
11. スーツ **sūtsu** suit
12. ベルト **beruto** belt
13. ズボン **zubon** pants
14. スプーン **supūn** spoon
15. ナイフ **naifu** knife
16. フォーク **fōku** fork
17. ハム **hamu** ham
18. ステーキ **sutēki** steak
19. パイナップル **painappuru** pineapple
20. バナナ **banana** banana
21. オレンジ **orenji** orange
22. メロン **meron** melon
23. サラダ **sarada** salad
24. ピザ **piza** pizza
25. チーズ **chīzu** cheese
26. ウイスキー **uisukī** whiskey
27. ビール **bīru** beer
28. ワイン **wain** wine
29. コーヒー **kōhī** coffee
30. ミルク **miruku** milk, cream
31. ジュース **jūsu** juice
32. コーラ **kōra** cola
33. グラス **gurasu** drinking glass

READING CHALLENGE 3: A Western-style Room

1. カレンダー **karendā** calendar
2. カーテン **kāten** curtain
3. スイッチ **suitchi** switch
4. ドア **doa** door
5. スタンド **sutando** desk lamp
6. ベッド **beddo** bed
7. パジャマ **pajama** pajamas
8. ベッドカバー **beddo-kabā** bedspread
9. クッション **kusshon** cushion
10. スリッパ **surippa** slippers
11. ギター **gitā** guitar
12. ボール **bōru** ball
13. カーペット **kāpetto** carpet
14. ケーキ **kēki** cake
15. アイスクリーム **aisu-kurīmu** ice cream
16. チョコレート **chokorēto** chocolate
17. ポット **potto** thermos jug
18. クーラー **kūrā** air conditioner
19. ヒーター **hītā** heater
20. テレビ **terebi** television
21. コンピューター **kompyūtā** computer
22. スピーカー **supīkā** speaker
23. コンセント **konsento** socket, outlet
24. コード **kōdo** cord
25. テーブル **tēburu** table
26. キャビネ **kyabine** bookshelf (an abbreviation of キャビネット, "cabinet")
27. ラケット **raketto** racke

COUNTRY INFORMATION

Country		Capital	
アメリカ	United States	ワシントン	Washington, DC
イギリス	United Kingdom	ロンドン	London
イタリア	Italy	ローマ	Rome
インド	India	デリー	Delhi
インドネシア	Indonesia	ジャカルタ	Jakarta
エジプト	Egypt	カイロ	Cairo
オーストラリア	Australia	キャンベラ	Canberra
オランダ	Netherlands	アムステルダム	Amsterdam
カナダ	Canada	オタワ	Ottawa
かんこく（韓国）	Republic of Korea	ソウル	Seoul
スイス	Switzerland	ベルン	Bern
タイ	Thailand	バンコク	Bangkok
ちゅうごく（中国）	China	ペキン（北京）	Beijing
ドイツ	Germany	ベルリン	Berlin
にほん（日本）	Japan	とうきょう（東京）	Tokyo
ニュージーランド	New Zealand	ウェリントン	Wellington
フィリピン	Philippines	マニラ	Manila
ブラジル	Brazil	ブラジリア	Brasilia
フランス	France	パリ	Paris
ベトナム	Vietnam	ハノイ	Hanoi
メキシコ	Mexico	メキシコシティ	Mexico City
ロシア	Russia	モスクワ	Moscow

Main Language(s)		Currency	
えいご	English	ドル	US dollar
えいご	English	ポンド	pound sterling
イタリアご	Italian	ユーロ	euro
ヒンディーご、えいご	Hindi, English	ルピー	rupee
インドネシアご	Indonesian	ルピア	rupiah
アラビアご	Arabic	エジプト・ポンド	Egyptian pound
えいご	English	オーストラリア・ドル	Australian dollar
オランダご、フリジアご	Dutch, Frisian	ユーロ	euro
えいご、フランスご	English, French	カナダ・ドル	Canadian dollar
かんこく（韓国）ご	Korean	ウォン	(South Korean) won
ドイツご、フランスご、イタリアご、ロマンシュご	German, French, Italian, Romansch	スイス・フラン	Swiss franc
タイご	Thai	バーツ	baht
ちゅうごく（中国）ご	Chinese	げん（元）	yuan
ドイツご	German	ユーロ	euro
にほん（日本）ご	Japanese	えん（円）	yen
えいご、マオリご	English, Maori	ニュジーランド・ドル	New Zealand dollar
フィリピンご、えいご	Filipino, English	フィリピン・ペソ	Philippine peso
ポルトガルご	Portuguese	レアル	real
フランスご	French	ユーロ	euro
ベトナムご	Vietnamese	ドン	dong
スペインご	Spanish	メキシコ・ペソ	Mexican peso
ロシアご	Russian	ルーブル	(Russian) ruble

An all-new edition of the all-time best-selling textbook

JAPANESE FOR BUSY PEOPLE: Revised 3rd Edition

Association for Japanese-Language Teaching (AJALT)

The leading textbook series for conversational Japanese has been redesigned, updated, and consolidated to meet the needs of today's students and businesspeople.

- Free CD with each text and workbook
- Edited for smoother transition between levels
- Hundreds of charming illustrations make learning Japanese easy
- Clear explanations of fundamental grammar

VOLUME 1 Teaches survival Japanese, or about one-third of the vocabulary and grammar typically introduced in beginner courses.

- **Japanese for Busy People I: Revised 3rd Edition, Romanized Version**
  Paperback, 296 pages, CD included ISBN: 978-1-56836-384-4
- **Japanese for Busy People I: Revised 3rd Edition, Kana Version**
  Paperback, 296 pages, CD included ISBN: 978-1-56836-385-1
- **Japanese for Busy People I: The Workbook for the Revised 3rd Edition**
  Paperback, 128 pages, CD included ISBN: 978-1-56836-399-8
- **Japanese for Busy People I: Teacher's Manual for the Revised 3rd Edition**
  Paperback, 152 pages, all in Japanese ISBN: 978-1-56836-400-1
- **Japanese for Busy People: Kana Workbook for the Revised 3rd Edition**
  Paperback, 104 pages, CD included ISBN: 978-1-56836-401-8
- **Japanese for Busy People I—App**
  Skill Practice on the Go app based on Volume I for iPhone, iPad, iPod and Android

VOLUME 2 Brings learners to the intermediate* level, enabling them to carry on basic conversations in everyday situations. (*upper beginners in Japan)

- **Japanese for Busy People II: Revised 3rd Edition**
  Paperback, 328 pages, CD included ISBN: 978-1-56836-386-8
- **Japanese for Busy People II: The Workbook for the Revised 3rd Edition**
  Paperback, 176 pages, CD included ISBN: 978-1-56836-402-5

VOLUME 3 Covers intermediate-level* Japanese. (*pre-intermediate in Japan)

- **Japanese for Busy People III: Revised 3rd Edition**
  Paperback, 328 pages, CD included ISBN: 978-1-56836-403-2
- **Japanese for Busy People III: The Workbook for the Revised 3rd Edition**
  Paperback, 144 pages, CD included ISBN: 978-1-56836-404-9
- **Japanese for Busy People II & III: Teacher's Manual for the Revised 3rd Edition**
  Paperback, 256 pages, all in Japanese ISBN: 978-1-56836-405-6